the
buzz

Other Books by Thelma Wells

❖ ❖ ❖

Bumblebees Fly Anyway:
Defying the Odds at Work and Home

The Best Devotions of Thelma Wells

What's Going On, Lord?

Girl, Have I Got Good News for You!

the
buzz

❖ ❀ ❖

7 Power-Packed
Scriptures
to Energize
Your Life

❖ ❀ ❖

Thelma Wells

W PUBLISHING GROUP
A Division of Thomas Nelson Publishers
Since 1798

www.wpublishinggroup.com

Published by W Publishing Group, a division of Thomas Nelson, Inc., P.O. Box 141000, Nashville, TN 37214.

W Publishing Group books may be purchased in bulk for educational, business, fundraising, or sales promotional use. For information, please e-mail SpecialMarkets@ThomasNelson.com.

Unless otherwise indicated, Scripture quotations used in this book are from the New King James Version (NKJV), copyright © 1982, Thomas Nelson, Inc. Used by permission.

Other Scripture passages are from these sources: The Holy Bible, New International Version (NIV). Copyright ©1973, 1978, 1984, International Bible Society. Used by permission of Zondervan Bible Publishers. *The Living Bible* (TLB) © 1971 Tyndale House Publishers, Wheaton, IL. The Holy Bible, New Living Translation (NLT), copyright © 1996 by Tyndale Charitable Trust. Used by permission of Tyndale House Publishers, Wheaton, IL. The King James Version (KJV) of the Bible. The New American Standard Bible (NASB), ©1960, 1977, 1995 by the Lockman Foundation. *The Message* (MSG). Copyright © 1993, 1994, 1995, 1996, 2000, 2001, 2002. Used by permission of NavPress Publishing Group.

Although personal incidents described in this volume are true, some details have been changed to protect identities.

Library of Congress Cataloging-in-Publication Data

Wells, Thelma, 1941-
    The buzz : seven scriptures to energize your life / Thelma Wells.
      p. cm.
    ISBN 0-8499-1827-8
    1. Christian life—Biblical teaching. I. Title.
    BS680.C47W45 2005
    248.4—dc22

                      2004025638

Printed in the United States of America
05 06 07 08 QW 9 8 7 6 5 4 3

Dedication and Thanks

❖ ❖ ❖

The Buzz is dedicated to the Holy Spirit, who guides me as I study his Word and lean on his understanding.

It's dedicated to the memory of my great-grandmother and great-grandfather, Sarah and William Harrell, who modeled for me what it looks like to study the Word and apply it to daily life.

It's dedicated to my "porch pals" with whom I work on the Women of Faith speaker team for their encouragement and insight as they reveal the Word of God week after week. A special thanks to Patsy Clairmont, who gave me the idea to call this book *The Buzz*.

It's dedicated to my children, grandchildren, and great-granddaughter, who I hope will follow the examples and legacy of their ancestors who loved the Word of God and meditated on it day and night.

And now some thank-yous . . .

To Debbie Wickwire of W Publishing Group for her patience during this process; to Mary Graham, the president of Women of Faith, for her input; and to Sue Ann Jones, my editor. What a joy to work with this team! Also, thanks and thumbs-up to Pat Mays, my administrative assistant, for all her help and for remembering where I'm supposed to be—and when!

❈ ❈ ❈

Contents

✤ ✤ ✤

He will yet fill your mouth with laughter and your lips with shouts of joy.

—Job 8:21 NIV

The LORD will fulfill his purpose for me; your love, O LORD, endures forever—do not abandon the works of your hands.

—Psalm 138:8 NIV

I can do all things through Christ who strengthens me.

—Philippians 4:13

Search me, O God, and know my heart; test me and know my anxious thoughts. See if there is any offensive way in me, and lead me in the way everlasting.

—Psalm 139:23–24 NIV

Foreword

❀ ❀ ❀

*T*helma Wells has been a blessing in my life. Her love, her smile, her laughter, and most importantly, her wisdom have been showered upon me and millions of women around the world. If you are in search of peace, hope, joy, or just a good laugh, you will find it all in *The Buzz*.

The Buzz is full of answers because it is full of the Word of God. It's a book that will breathe life into any dead situation, so go ahead and enjoy it and buy one for a friend because when you share *The Buzz*, you're sharing life. Thelma Wells, with a "sista-girl" delivery that is second to none, always encourages everyone, everywhere, to be all they can be—and the message continues in *The Buzz*.

—CeCe Winans

I

Buzzin'
with the Love
of the Lord

*G*irl, I've gotta tell you something.

I'm not kidding. I've really *got* to tell you this, or I think I'll explode. I can't keep it in. These words are bubblin' up inside me, and I want to share them with you so bad I'm just—well, I'm just *buzzin'* with excitement. Hmmmmm, mmmmmmm, mmmmm! That's the only way to describe it. It feels like my insides are vibrating harder than a heavy-duty washing machine on spin cycle. I feel like one of those little honeybees that's found a feast of flowers and is trembling with excitement and doing that dance bees do to tell the rest of the hive where they can find the good stuff too.

Now, here's the good stuff *I* want to tell *you*: God is real, and he loves you and me like nobody's business! In fact, he loves us so much, he sent his only Son to earth to *die* for us. Can you believe it? Well, if you can, I've got even better news: Jesus is coming back to earth one of these days, and he's gonna take us believers to heaven to live with him *forever*. Did you get that? For-EV-uh! Honey, it just doesn't get any better than that.

What's that you say? You already *knew* that? Well, for heaven's sake, how can you just sit there reading? Don't you wanna jump up and dance like a honeybee and shout, "Hallelujah!" every time you think about it? Go ahead. Put the book down—just for a second, mind you! You come right back here as soon as you're finished— then lift up your hands and say, "Thank you, Lord! I praise you, Father! Glory to you, O God most high."

When I think that the One who created the universe—the One who hung the moon, ignited the sun, and flung the stars across the sky—also created *me*, I'm overwhelmed with wonder. When I realize the horrific sacrifice Jesus made for me, I'm moved to tears. And when I remember that there's a mansion waiting for me in heaven, I'm excited beyond words.

Well, no, now that I think about it, I guess I've always got something to say. I make my living these days by speaking and sharing God's love and promises with audiences around the world. But before I head out to remind others what God has *done* for us, I always want to know what God, our Creator, has *said* to us. So I study his Word. I read the Bible and soak up the teaching in it. I immerse myself in the Scriptures, and I fill my head with its promises and teachings so that whenever I'm confronted with a challenging situation, a difficult choice, a personal setback, I can find in my memory a lifeline of scriptural guidance and encouragement that will help me take the next step.

This practice began for me when I was a child and, as many children do, I memorized two of the most treasured passages in the Bible: the Lord's Prayer (found in Matthew 6:9–13) and the Twenty-third Psalm.

My beloved great-grandmother taught me to pull those passages from my memory and recite them in stressful situations to find both peace and strength. I've followed her advice all my life. I've hurriedly whispered those words to myself in no telling how many far-flung airports, hospital waiting rooms, conference arenas, business offices, hotel rooms, and government offices. I've closed my eyes and recited those comforting passages as I've waited for the phone to ring, waited for a child to come home, waited for a decision to be made, waited for the air to smooth out and the turbulence to end at thirty thousand feet. And every time I recite them, I can feel my worry easing, my blood pressure dropping, my muscles relaxing.

The experience teaches me again and again the truth and power of God's Word. Psalm 54:4 (NIV) says, "Surely God is my help; the Lord is the one who sustains me." And the Thelma Wells translation might add, "Mmmmmmm, mmmmmm, mmmmmm! Thank you, Jesus!" In times of stress, I've found that precious, remembered passages of Scripture create a lifeline that links me to God's constant presence and sustains me with his boundless love.

I spend a lot of time reading the Bible and studying its truths. If I'm not reading it, I'm listening to it on tape or CD; these days you can even *watch* the Bible on DVDs! In this book, I'd like to share seven of the special Bible passages I've stocked in the scriptural pantry of my mind as I've studied God's Word. These are verses that have brought me comfort, guidance, and encouragement as I've passed through sunshine and shadow on my life's journey. You know, seven is a heavenly number, the number of completion, and each of the seven passages I share here has been especially helpful in my life in celebrating joy, and in seeking purpose, perseverance, prayer, hope, faith, or peace. Throughout these chapters I'll tell you how God's Word has helped and inspired me—and others—in all sorts of situations.

You'll find lots of other beautiful portions of Scripture woven through this book too in addition to the focus passages. The Bible is an extraordinary book of history, poetry, drama, biography, religion, letters, prophecy, and a whole lot more. My goal is to help you make its beautiful passages and promises a part of your everyday life. I hope you'll keep the focus passages handy so you can retrieve them whenever they're needed. Consider writing them down on index cards to carry around in your purse so that, whenever you're stuck in a waiting room or idling in the carpool line, you can take them out and commit them to memory. Or take along this little book as you ingest these passages and make them a part of your life. You'll find the focus passages collected in one place at the back; see the part titled "Now, What Were Those Seven Scriptures Again?" As you spend time in God's Word yourself, you'll probably find many more passages to "adopt" into your personal arsenal so they're handy whenever you're confronted with daily challenges and decisions.

When you're finished with this book, I hope you feel energized and filled with such enthusiasm for praising God and trusting in his Word that you just can't keep it to yourself. My wish is that you'll soon be buzzin' along with me, filled to overflowing with the love of the Lord and his Word.

2

Joy

Congenitally Gifted
with Giggling

*He will yet fill your mouth with laughter and
your lips with shouts of joy.*

—*Job 8:21 NIV*

$\mathscr{P}$eople often ask me, "Why are you so happy all the
time?" Well, I'm happy because when I wake up in the
morning, I don't read my name in the obituaries! I'm
alive, and I've been given the gift of one more day. Life
is precious, and every day is a new opportunity; I want to
wring all the joy out of it that I possibly can.

Now, admittedly, someone with this demeanor often
stands out in the crowd (especially if the crowd is feeling
cranky that day). I once overheard a woman ask my

daughter Vikki, "Is your mother like this all the time?" She meant did I laugh and seem to enjoy life all the time.

If Vikki were one to roll her eyes, she might have rolled them then. "Yes," she replied with a sigh. "She makes me tired. I can't even have a bad day around her. You know, some days I just want to feel sorry for myself, but you can't be around Mama and be sad for long."

Well, I took that as a compliment! I'm glad she can't have a bad day around me. Why would anybody want to have a bad day anyway? As the Bible says, each day comes with its own trouble (see Matthew 6:34). Why add to it by going around with a scowl on your face and an ice cube in your heart?

At my age, I can't afford to give over a whole day to worry, sadness, and anxiety. I only have about 50 more years left to live (assuming I reach my goal of living to be 120), and I want those years to be happy and productive. While I'm here I want to make the world a better place, and if I can't make the *whole* world a better place, then I want to at least make my immediate vicinity happier. Worry and bitterness do nothing but bring our spirits down and cause us to look and act tired and worn out all the time. And those sentiments are contagious. But so is joy. If you're going to spread something, spread joy!

Spreading the Joy

This laughing and smiling habit of mine wasn't something that happened after I was grown. No, I've always been this way. I guess you could say I'm congenitally gifted with giggling. In fact, when I was six years old and in the first grade at J. W. Ray Elementary in Dallas, I won a smile contest sponsored by a local dentist. I still have the newspaper clipping showing me, with a huge smile of course, holding the huge loving-cup trophy the school won for sponsoring the contest.

My husband's Aunt Doretha Cashaw, who's like an aunt and mentor to me too, tells people, talking about me, "That gal laughs all the time. She laughs at her own self. When she's on the stage, she'll say something she thinks is funny, and she'll laugh at herself and bring everybody else along with her. Sometimes what she says ain't even funny, but they laugh 'cause she's laughin'. That gal is crazy!"

I'm not the only laughter-loving member of the family. Our son, George, has always had a keen sense of humor. There's never a dull moment when he's around, muttering his George-isms and telling his crazy stories. And I'm happy to report that George's infant son, Philip, seems to have the joy gene too. He has a wide smile and a hearty laugh that shakes his little plump body so much he topples over onto his stomach. And when someone rolls him upright again, he's still laughing. One of my granddaughters, Alaya, laughs about everything too. I like to think these precious grandbabies have inherited their grandmother's joyful personality. Surely it's one of the most valuable gifts I could pass on to them.

There's just something contagious about laughter, something infectious about a joyful attitude. Start laughing in a room full of people, and before you know it, you're surrounded by laughter. Marilyn Meberg is an expert at that bit of magic. She tells the story of being bored to tears when she was a little girl picking strawberries all alone in a strawberry patch. There was nothing to laugh at and no one to laugh with, but Marilyn decided to laugh anyway. She began with a reserved chuckle and soon worked herself up to full-blown guffawing. She laughed and laughed and laughed, and before she knew it, the strawberries were picked and she was trotting back to the house, giggling all the way.

She can still conjure up a laugh at the drop of a hat, and it's impossible not to laugh with her once she starts. I've seen Marilyn turn a quiet, reserved audience of more than ten thousand women into a roaring, knee-slapping, hilarious hall of belly-laughers. In the process they're learning that there's value in laughing, even when there's nothing to laugh about. Joy and laughter are gifts from God that help heal us from the turmoil of life.

Women of Faith originated with founder Stephen Arterburn's idea of sharing the gift of laughter and the love of God with women around the country. As he sat in an arena listening to some international speakers, laughing heartily and having the time of his life, Steve thought, *Wouldn't it be wonderful if we could fill churches with women by bringing in funny Christian speakers who could entertain them while giving them God's wisdom to live by?* The first year's conferences were titled "Joyful Journey," and the tour, which has outgrown churches and now fills large arenas, has been journeying joyfully around North America ever since. Now, nearly one decade and two and a half million women later, one of the most encouraging (and most frequent) remarks we hear on the tour comes from women who say, "I've never laughed so much in all my life. I didn't know I needed to laugh. Thank you."

Whatever Life Holds—Choose Joy

Now, laughter may come naturally to some of us. But that doesn't mean our lives are full of joyful situations. In fact, some of our lives are full of sorry "stuff" that rivals the trials of Job. How many times have you thought of yourself as "Jobette" because you were going through stuff that you did not order and could not send back by FedEx? Storms may have swept through your life and carried you to the depths of despair as you endured broken relationships, wayward children, catastrophic illness or injury, church rivalry, job loss, eating disorders, emotional instability, a loved one's death, financial setbacks, legal issues, public ridicule, immoral conduct, or no telling what else.

You're nodding your head, aren't you? Everybody's had some kind of bad stuff in her life; I sure have. And nobody's saying we're supposed to laugh every time another punch finds its mark. Ecclesiastes 3:1, 4 (NIV) says, "There is a time for everything . . . : a time to weep and a time to laugh, a time to mourn and a time to dance." The important thing is to remember, during those times of weeping and mourning, the promise that God "will yet fill your mouth with laughter and your lips with shouts of joy." Whisper it to yourself when you find yourself at trouble's doorstep: "God will yet fill my mouth with laughter and my lips with shouts of joy." Let that promise of joy-yet-to-come be your strength during the hard times.

The more you practice this attitude, the more powerful it is and the faster it pops into your mind when you're confronted with difficulties. During my own crises and trials, and I've certainly had my share, I've learned to reach into my innermost human computer and pull out scriptural data that can help me remember what God has done for me in the past and what he has promised to do for me in the future. I can document the trials he has pulled me through, and, reviewing that history, I can anticipate where he might be taking me, even in the middle of trouble.

When something devastating happens, we rightfully mourn for what we have lost, whether it's our health, our financial well-being, a loved one who has died, or some other grievous situation. But we remind ourselves that someday, when the time to mourn has passed and our grief has eased, God will once again "fill our mouths with laughter and our lips with shouts of joy."

Job's Way of Surviving Catastrophes

The Old Testament character Job had a remarkable tenacity for maintaining that flicker of joy while he was going through one heinous loss after another. He had been a healthy, wealthy, strong, and respected husband and father, and a pillar of the community. But suddenly horrible things started happening to him. He lost his health, his children, his wealth, and his friends, and finally his wife told him to curse God and die. To Job, there was no reason for these events. He had always been faithful to God, and he continued in that faithfulness despite all the calamities that occurred.

Job didn't know about the conversation God had with Satan, who claimed that Job only followed God because of all the good things God had given him. Of course God knew that wasn't true, and he allowed Satan to take away everything Job held dear so that his steadfast faithfulness would be revealed. And that's exactly what happened. Job lost everything except his faith in God, and that faith not only sustained *him* through the hard times, but his example also has inspired millions of us believers for thousands of years since then as his story, recorded in the Bible, has been handed down from generation to generation.

The words in the verse we're focusing on in this chapter actually came from one of Job's so-called friends, Bildad the Shuhite. Bildad, along with the other two friends, assumed that Job's troubles were due to his sins.

All Job had to do, they assured him, was repent of those sins and then everything would be hunky-dory. But Job argued that he *hadn't* sinned; he *hadn't* done anything to displease God.

Bildad didn't believe Job. He still thought Job's troubles had occurred because he had turned away from God. Bildad warned, "That's what happens to all who forget God—all their hopes come to nothing. They hang their life from one thin thread, they hitch their fate to a spider web. One jiggle and the thread breaks, one jab and the web collapses" (Job 8:13–15 MSG). Bildad falsely accused Job, but obviously he did have some things right. And he was equally correct a little later when he told Job that someday God would once again "fill your mouth with laughter and your lips with shouts of joy."

God let Satan take everything away from Job, but when Satan had to concede defeat, God gave it all back—and more. Job died not knowing about the conversation between God and the devil. But he found out that knowing God was more important than understanding his circumstances. That's how Job survived the hard times, and that's how we survive our trials today. God allowed Job to go through turmoil, but God never left him to go through it alone. He was always there, giving him strength. He does the same for us today, and his presence provides that flicker of joy deep in our heart that never goes away, no matter how difficult our circumstances.

The Lesson of the Bee

Joy, happiness, and laughter are different things that are sometimes, but not always, related. Happiness is temporary, while the kind of joy we're discussing here is a permanent trait. It may go dormant occasionally, but while we maintain our close relationship with our Creator, it's always there, glowing in the darkness.

Laughter can be an expression of happiness or of joy— or of something else entirely. You can laugh without real joy. In fact, sometimes laughter is an expression of embarrassment or awkwardness. In studying audiences around the world, I've decided that sometimes people laugh because they don't know what else to do. For example, I attended a conference where a speaker used some off-color language. The audience laughed uncomfortably each time the words were uttered. The remarks weren't funny, and the words were unexpected, especially in that setting; in response the audience chuckled as though embarrassed by what was being said.

You can laugh without feeling joyful. On the other hand, you can't have real joy without being able to laugh at yourself and others and at the situations you land in. A joyful person buzzes through each life experience optimistically like a honeybee buzzing around the backyard, looking for a flower.

If you know anything about me, you know that I'm fascinated with bees. That's one reason this book has "Bee Facts" sprinkled through it like morsels of pollen hidden here and there. I hope these little bits of information about the bee and how hard it works and how

> *bee fact*
>
> ❀ ❀ ❀
>
> In the time it takes you to blink, a flying bee flaps its wings 250 times.
>
> —Elin Kelsey,
> *Bees*

it copes with challenges will make you think about how you're responding to the circumstances you find yourself in from time to time. When I look at the bee, I see some remarkable similarities between us humans and this fascinating little creature, starting with the fact that we both have the same Creator.

I've become such an admirer of bees that I've adopted

one, the bumblebee, as my personal logo (more about that in the next chapter). I wear a bumblebee pin every day of the week to remind me that in Christ I can *bee* my best, no matter what my circumstances are. You see, there was a time when scientists proclaimed that it was aerodynamically impossible for the bumblebee to fly. Its body is too big, and its wings are too short, these experts announced. Fortunately, as I like to say, nobody told that fool it can't fly! So off it goes, buzzin' around all over the place.

In the same way, there were times in my life when I was told that I couldn't do something because of my race or my sex or my lack of experience or some other disqualifier. But every chance I got, I proved those people wrong. That's why I love the bumblebee. However, I'm equally enchanted with the honeybee, the bumblebee's cousin, because it too seems to do the impossible.

Honeybees sort themselves out into different job categories, apparently progressing through the various stages as they age; as far as we can tell, there's no arguing over who does what in the hive. They are loyal to their queen and selfless in their dedication to their fellow bees. Newly hatched bees work inside the dark hive at various tasks; then, in the last stage of the bee's life, it goes forth into the sunlight.

To gather pollen and nectar, the forager bees travel

great distances and have an uncanny sense of direction. They carry enormous loads and also show incredible endurance. And while I've never personally interviewed any honeybees, I just can't help but believe that they have a joyful personality. If bees could say anything else but "Buzzzzzzzz," I think they would probably fly out of the hive each morning singing "Whistle While You Work."

---

bee fact

For her weight and size, a honeybee is said to fly faster and farther than any other winged creature. She is the opposite of her cousin, the cumbersome bumblebee who, according to aeronautical flight criteria, has been proved incapable of flight.

–William Longgood,
The Queen Must Die and Other Affairs of Bees and Men

Their whole life is consumed with storing up food for the coming winter and for perpetuating the hive. So I'm thinking if they had a favorite Scripture verse it might be Proverbs 15:15 (NIV): "The cheerful heart has a continual feast."

I'm probably being silly. But there's a lot to be admired

in the honeybee. Look at the never-ending toil it faces each day; bees are amazing, inspiring creatures. As far as I can tell, there are basically two stages in a honeybee's life. Either it works tirelessly in the total darkness of the hive, tending the young, building perfectly hexagonal cells (with a slight downward tilt so the honey doesn't run out), grooming the queen, serving on guard duty, or providing climate control by fanning its wings or huddling with other bees in a trembling clump for warmth — or it flies back and forth over great distances in the heat of the day, constantly carrying heavy loads of pollen and nectar between the blossoms and the hive.

I could be reading its body language all wrong, but despite all this hard work the honeybee just seems to exude a joyfully enthusiastic attitude. For instance, when a honeybee discovers a new source of food, it zips back to the hive, all atwitter, and then, buzzing with excitement, it does that special honeybee dance that tells the other bees just where the banquet can be found.

That's how I feel when the joy of the Lord fills my heart to overflowing—which is most of the time. I work hard too, just like the honeybee. But that godly gift of joy just sets me all atwitter, and without any conscious effort, it bubbles up out of me in the form of laughter. Then I can't wait to tell all those around me where they can find the banquet of God's goodness too.

A Joy Not of This World

Laughter must be pretty important to God or he wouldn't have spent so much time talking about it. Depending on which version of the Bible you're studying, the word *laughter* appears about forty times. One of my favorite laughter verses is part of the Old Testament story of Abraham and his wife, Sarah, who gave birth when Abraham was one hundred years old and Sarah herself was well past her childbearing years. When their son Isaac was miraculously born, Sarah said, "God has brought me laughter, and everyone who hears about this will laugh with me" (Genesis 21:6 NIV).

Frankly, I don't know too many women today who would think it was funny to have a new baby in their old age. Having a hundred-year-old husband to care for would be hard enough, let alone an infant too! But God had promised Abraham and Sarah a family, and when that promise was fulfilled, Sarah laughed with delight. I'm guessing that joy-filled attitude worked like a daily dose of vitamins, keeping Sarah going so that she could be a good mother to her son and a loving wife to her husband despite their increasing age. She knew the wisdom expressed in Proverbs 17:22 (KJV): "A merry heart doeth good like a medicine."

Always trying to be obedient, I too try to fill that prescription every chance I get and take a huge dose of laughter. One of the ways I do that is with a group of my friends who, over the past five decades, have gotten together periodically just to laugh and enjoy each other. We grew up in the same church, know many of the same people, and have watched each other's careers, marriages, children, and aging adventures. We know each other very well, and when we schedule one of these get-togethers, we're laughing before we ever get to where we're gathering. We greet each other with laughter before we even say hello. We laugh while we're hugging, and we laugh while we're talking. Sometimes someone will ask, "What's so funny?" and we all burst out laughing all over again.

It's not that anything is *that* funny. It's just that being together is a delightful time for us, and it "doeth good like a medicine." After one of these gatherings, we all feel relaxed and purged of many of our cares. For some of us, hearty laughter is the most strenuous aerobic exercise we get!

The joy we feel in each other's presence isn't a shallow, temporary thing. It's an abiding feeling that has been developing throughout the half-century many of us have known each other. In the same way, the joy we have as Christians is more than a temporary experience. There's an old Negro spiritual hymn that describes "this joy that I have" as something the world didn't give and the world can't take away. This joy is a rock-solid promise that anchors our attitude and confirms our belief that God is our close and constant Friend (see Proverbs 18:24) who will be with us through the bad stuff here on earth and who will welcome us one day into paradise, where we'll live with him forever. As C. S. Lewis said, "Joy is the serious business of heaven."

Occasionally we may feel overwhelmed by anger, bitterness, or sorrow, but those harsh emotions cannot extinguish the true, God-given joy that was placed in our heart by the Holy Spirit the moment we accepted Jesus as Lord and Savior. It may be temporarily overshadowed by raging hormones and hostile feelings, but when we regain control and begin to think about God's goodness and love, the joy re-exerts itself, and before we know it, our negative emotions have evaporated as once again our mouth is filled with laughter and our lips with shouts of joy. Our facial expressions change. Our aggressive body language stands down. Our demeanor sweetens. God's joy is powerful. Even in the most stressful situations, if we allow it to work within us, we find a way to follow the instructions of the apostle Paul, who instructed the Philippians, "Rejoice in the Lord alway; and again I say, Rejoice" (4:4 KJV).

What's the Buzz?

He will yet fill your mouth with laughter and your lips with shouts of joy.

—Job 8:21

Joy and laughter are God-given gifts that help us live less stressful, more productive lives. When you have nothing to laugh about, laugh anyway; soon you'll feel the healing power of joy and laughter bringing new energy and life to your weary, frustrating day.

3

Purpose

In Christ,
You Can *Bee* Your Best

The LORD will fulfill his purpose for me; your love, O LORD, endures forever—do not abandon the works of your hands.

—Psalm 138:8 NIV

I was forty years old when I discovered my calling in life. That's not to say I was floundering around, unemployed and unmotivated, during the years leading up to that discovery. I had worked hard and overcome a lot of challenges to get a college degree and then to forge a career in banking. Later I had developed courses and a textbook for training other bank employees in opening new accounts and in customer service, and I was busy presenting that training in American Institute of Banking seminars to bank employees around the state. It was a rewarding career, and I enjoyed it, but I always wanted to be better at what I was doing. I prayed and asked God to give me a message I could leave with my students that they would remember long after they had forgotten my name and face.

Then, one Sunday evening, God showed me how he would grant that desire. He took my developing sense of purpose, my desire to share a message of personal impact, and he cranked things up a notch. That night I happened to wear a little bumblebee pin to evening church services. My friend Mary Jo Evans, who is quite a bit more animated than I am (if that's possible!), noticed the little pin as we entered the church together, and she said to me, "Thelma, that surrrrrrre is a pretty bee! Every time you wearrrrrrrr that bee, remember: you can *beeeeeee* the best of whatever you want to be!"

From that moment on, I've claimed the bumblebee as my logo. And I've used that theme—*bee* the best of whatever you want to be—to inspire and encourage audiences all over the world. I began this new aspect of my career by adding a ten-minute "pep talk" to the last night of class each semester that I was teaching the banking course.

Now, that class was completely secular, so I couldn't share the gospel with those students, but I did my best to encourage them to seek out a purpose for their lives and pursue it with everything they had.

The response was amazing. Right away people started asking me to come to their events and organizations to deliver that motivational message. Each time I spoke, I felt an amazing sense of fulfillment and satisfaction. Looking back, I realized that everything I had done to that point in my life had been preparing me for what God had planned for me since the foundation of the world.

As a little girl I was given opportunities to speak in my church, school, and community. When I was older, I entered oratorical contests and learned speeches to present for special occasions. In college I took oral communications in business and listened to all the speakers I could. I was interested in their speaking style and in what they said. Then I became a banker, and after taking the mandatory training course, I realized I could do a better job of presenting the information than the current instructors were doing. So I developed my own book and curriculum, and I started teaching the course myself. I noticed that many people in my classes were timid and intimidated by taking tests and speaking up in class. That's when I asked

God to give me a message that would encourage these students to step beyond their perceived limitations and be the best they could be. And *that's* when Mary Jo noticed my bumblebee pin and gave me the words that became the theme of my message of inspiration and encouragement.

The Pieces of God's Puzzle

Isn't God good? Isn't it amazing how, while we're in the midst of what may seem like ho-hum, ordinary, everyday routines and careers, we're actually living out pieces of the puzzle that will eventually create the big picture God has planned for our lives? The important thing to remember, while we're trudging along through every ordinary day, is to make ourselves available and open to God. Take the verse at the beginning of this chapter and personalize it. Start every day with the request, "Dear Father, please fulfill your purpose for me; your love, O Lord, endures forever—do not abandon the works of your hands. Put me to use in your service, Lord, wherever that service might be today."

I get e-mail messages and letters from people who are desperately looking for their purpose in life, people who feel unfulfilled, people wondering why they were born, people asking, Is this all there is to life, just getting up in the morning, going to work, coming home, doing the chores, eating, sleeping, watching television, and starting all over again with the same routine the next day?

I tell them they need an attitude adjustment. They need to realize that their daily routine is connected with their purpose in life. It's how we fulfill our purpose *daily*. First of all, remember that Scripture tells us, "Whatever you do, do your work heartily, as for the Lord rather than for men" (Colossians 3:23 NASB). If you're washing dishes, wash those dishes as though the Lord himself were gonna eat off of them. If you're piloting an airplane, pilot it as though God himself was one of your passengers. If you're caring for children, give them the kind of focused, loving care you would give to God's own kids (which they are!).

Put Some Hallelujah! in the Humdrum

When you look at everyday life as a gift from God and as your gift to him—and as one little piece of the puzzle of purpose that God has planned for you from the beginning of the universe—then each day can be an exciting occasion for discovering the divine appointments God has for you.

I don't know what I'd do if I couldn't look forward to something exciting each day. Now, I'm not talking about drama-queen excitement but about activities that keep the spark in my life. I have to work at my purpose for it to be successful. My days are similar to this: I wake up with Jesus on my mind and spend some quiet time either in the bedroom, the bathroom, or the kitchen praising God (quietly so I don't disturb my husband's morning). Sometimes I find myself praying for him as he goes about his morning routine. Even though we pray together, we also have our private prayer time. You know, we women can do a lot of things at one time! So sometimes I'm praying and preparing my day's agenda at the same time. And as I prepare, I become filled with anticipation, thinking about the people and events God is going to bring into my life that day.

> ### bee fact
>
> ❀ ❀ ❀
>
> Looking after the infant bees, called grubs, is no easy task for the worker bees. There may be thousands of grubs in a hive, and each one has to be fed thirteen hundred times each day.
>
> —Elin Kelsey,
> *Bees*

One of my most productive daily prayers asks God to "fulfill his purpose for me." I pray, "Your love, O Lord, endures forever—do not abandon the works of your hands." I want to keep his hand on me all the day long. Then I pray, "Father, open the doors I need to walk through today, and close the doors I don't. Put people in my way that I need to talk to today, and get people out of my way who might distract me from your purpose for me. Show me what you want me to do today. And please, Sir, don't let me waste time!"

I start by doing the highest priority things first, whatever they are. I try not to put off the things I don't want to do if they're the things I *should* do. One of my favorite priorities each day is checking on my children and grandchildren. I also try to make time to do some of the things my husband wants us to do together. I'm thankful that he is my staunchest supporter. We both stay busy with our own work and activities, but we make sure that we schedule time to connect with each other. I also work with my staff, catch up on my writing assignments, study my Bible, run errands, check my e-mail, pray with people who call or come by, and make phone calls. If I have a deadline that day, I devote my time to completing that task. And although these activities may seem ho-hum and humdrum, I do them as though I'm doing them for the Lord, believing that when I'm walking in his will I'm fulfilling his purpose for me.

Most of these activities can happen whether I'm at home or traveling. Since that day when I adopted the bumblebee as my logo and started adding motivational and inspirational speaking to my career, I have felt a great sense of fulfillment and satisfaction. The results I started seeing in the people I spoke to were amazing. It was as if I had found my home after years of wandering; in fact, I had found my God-given purpose.

My sense of fulfillment has multiplied enormously as I've been given opportunities to speak to Christian groups, including Women of Faith. Now I don't have to motivate my audiences by simply encouraging them to find their own way to "*bee* the best" of whatever they choose to be. In Christian settings, I'm free to put this motivation in its most powerful form. I can say, "In *Christ* and *for* Christ, you can *bee* the best in whatever work God gives you to do."

The variety of speaking invitations that come in are truly amazing. Recently I was asked to speak at a religious conference for the Women of Islam. As I pondered whether to go, I was reminded of another occasional prayer of mine: "Lord, please give me opportunities to witness for you."

Then I was reminded of my belief that God wanted me to consider every speaking invitation as an opportunity to proclaim a word for him. I accepted the invitation and began my talk by saying, "I greet you in the name of Jehovah Yahweh, my Creator and God, and in the name of *Yahushua*, Jesus Christ, my Lord and Savior."

Afterward many of the women thanked me for a powerful message. I have come to realize that all people have been born with an innate desire to be in fellowship with their Creator. The world is looking for God in so many different places. It can be scary to address those with different beliefs, but God will be with us as we reach out with the gospel, seeking to fulfill his purpose for us.

Fulfilling God's Purpose

For twenty-two years, I have believed in my heart that my *purpose* is helping people become their best in Christ. My *calling*, the vocation through which I fulfill that purpose, is speaking to audiences around the world with that message. This calling has become a passion for me. I work at it day and night, and in general I'm on a plane traveling to speaking engagements forty weeks of the year. I've been keeping this pace for a long time, and I'm not tired yet. I'm energized to think the Lord is fulfilling his purpose for me. And I'm continually intrigued by and seeking out new and different ways of communicating to people that in Christ they can *bee* the best at whatever they are doing.

Sales and management expert Tom Thiss says, "Having a purpose is the difference between making a living and making a life." My experience verifies what he's saying. For many years, I made a *living* out of teaching and speaking to audiences about banking practices. But when I discovered how I could use my teaching and speaking skills to fulfill the *purpose* I perceived that God had planned for me, my career took on new meaning, new depth, new passion. Today I am living out my belief that each of us was sent to earth for a purpose. It's all part of our relationship with our Creator and our willingness to become subject to the perfect will of God through Jesus Christ.

Now, that's not to say everything rolls along perfectly in my life day in and day out. No way! I get headaches, flat tires, and snags in my pantyhose just like people who *aren't* living out God's purpose in their lives. There have been a few times when I've had a speaking engagement that did not go well and I was disappointed with my performance. I spoke at a church's women's conference the first year it was organized; I gave God all the glory and allowed him to speak through me. It was a wonderful experience for all of us. When I was invited back again the next year, I was so afraid of not doing as well as I'd done the first time that I nervously concentrated more on what I was going to say than on what God wanted me to say. I didn't spend enough time in prayer and in the Word before the event. I hadn't asked God to fulfill his purpose for me as I spoke to those women.

After I spoke at the conference the second time, I knew I hadn't done as well as the year before. I couldn't pull my thoughts together; I got off the subject. I was a mess! People told me the speech was good, but I wanted to crawl under a bush because I knew better. I was angry with myself for trying to make a name for myself instead of depending on God.

I arrived home from that conference depressed. God had not shone through me to those women. Before I even unpacked my suitcase, I fell on my knees and asked God what happened. In my spirit, the Lord told me I had not asked him what he wanted me to do. In my spirit he reminded me that I represent not only Thelma Wells but, more importantly, I represent Jesus Christ.

When God and I finished our conversation, I asked myself, *What was I thinking, not asking God to orchestrate my message? Why did I think I could do that on my own when he had been my Guide and Counselor all the past times I spoke to audiences?* And my answer to myself was, *Thelma, you were looking inward, not upward. You were self-serving and self-seeking, not God-seeking. You were arrogant and proud, not humble and meek. You were acting in the flesh with a carnal mind, not in the Spirit with the mind of God. So there, Miss Honey, you are not all that and a bag of chips. Your chips are rank and stale. Get over yourself, 'cause by yourself and without God, you ain't nothin', girl!*

Oh, I really let myself have it! I spent the next few days analyzing myself in the light of God's Word and studying what had gone wrong. After such a severe reprimanding, I needed some encouragement as I flew off to another engagement. So on the plane, I turned to Romans 8 and found just what I needed—renewal for my purpose and calling:

> Those who think they can do it on their own end up obsessed with measuring their own moral muscle but never get around to exercising it in real life. Those who trust God's action in them find that

God's Spirit is in them—living and breathing God! Obsession with self in these matters is a dead end; attention to God leads us out into the open, into a spacious, free life. Focusing on the self is the opposite of focusing on God. Anyone completely absorbed in self ignores God, ends up thinking more about self than God. That person ignores who God is and what he is doing. And God isn't pleased at being ignored.

But if God himself has taken up residence in your life, you can hardly be thinking more of yourself than of him. (vv. 5–9 MSG)

And then I read the last two verses of chapter 8, which always get me stirred up and leave me buzzin' like a bee, happy to be reminded of God's love and grace:

I'm absolutely convinced that nothing—nothing living or dead, angelic or demonic, today or tomorrow, high or low, thinkable or unthinkable—absolutely *nothing* can get between us and God's love because of the way that Jesus our Master has embraced us. (MSG)

When I read this beloved passage on the airplane that

day, everything in me said *YES!* I was *buzzed!* I wanted to jump up and shout out loud to my fellow passengers, "God loves me! He's not angry with me. He called me to my vocation as a speaker for his glory, and he wants me to ask him for help with my speaking assignments. But when I mess up, he doesn't say, 'You're FIRED!' He uses me in spite of myself. I am in his good graces, and he is going to greatly increase my ability to trust him as I follow my passion and answer my calling. Thank you, God! You are a great Daddy and wonderful Father and an awesome God."

Fortunately, I was able to contain myself. Otherwise, I'm sure the sky marshals would have been reaching for their handcuffs, thinking I was trying to take over the plane. And at that point, I probably *would* have taken it over—and turned it into a praise flight!

bee fact

❀ ❀ ❀

Bees are, above all, creatures of the future. The bee's today is made up of anticipating tomorrow.

—William Longgood,
The Queen Must Die and Other Affairs of Bees and Men

Becoming More Like Jesus

Why does God help us up again and again when we stumble and fall? To help us become more like his Son, Jesus! That point was reinforced when I heard my pastor, Leroy R. Armstrong Jr., teach from this same powerful chapter in Romans at our church, St. John Missionary Baptist in Dallas. He began by reading Romans 8:28 (NLT), another one of those beloved passages we all repeat when we need to encourage ourselves in not-too-good situations: "And we know that God causes everything to work together for the good of those who love God and are called according to his purpose for them."

But Pastor Armstrong said that we often fail to read the next verses, 29 and 30, which have as much or maybe more significance than verse 28. Those two verses tell us that God foreknew all of us and predestined us to become like his Son. Here's how it reads in *The Living Bible* paraphrase:

> For from the very beginning God decided that those who came to him—and all along he knew who would—should become like his Son, so that his Son would be the First, with many brothers. And having chosen us, he called us to come to him;

and when we came, he declared us "not guilty," filled us with Christ's goodness, gave us right standing with himself, and promised us his glory.

The key words in this passage are "become like his Son." How can we do that? Only by surrendering our lives to his Son's perfect will for us and by fully realizing that we are not running anything in our lives. Whatever God allows in his children's lives is for one purpose: to draw us closer to his Son. He wants to build our confidence in his Son to the extent that we depend on him for *everything*.

Why do bad things happen to good people? To help them become like his Son.

Why did I forget to consult God before my speaking engagement for the second year of the women's conference? Well, for starters, because I'm only human. But God used this embarrassing experience to help me become more like his Son. If I had not made that mistake, I would never have known how costly it was. Sure, people said I was good, but I knew the truth: I *was* good, but I had not allowed God to work through me, so I wasn't the best I could be.

Thank God he doesn't need our permission to work in our lives. That's a relief! But he does expect us to yield to him and follow his directions in every aspect of our lives.

Turning the Pages of Our Life

As God's children, our lives unfold daily like pages in a book. Each circumstance is a different chapter. Each page is a new opportunity to live out God's plan for us. I believe that nothing is coincidental; everything in our life is under the providence of God. Jeremiah said, "I know, God, that mere mortals can't run their own lives, that men and women don't have what it takes to take charge of life" (10:23 MSG). From the day of our birth to the day of our death, we must remember the wisdom of Psalm 37:23: "The steps of a good man are ordered by the LORD."

God's will is *upon* us in all the things that happen in our life—in the hurt and the sorrow and in the joy and the peace. As I turn the pages of my life, I see chapters I could never have completed on my own. It was the sovereign hand of God that caused those chapters to be written. He was working things out for me before the foundation of the world, before my mama and daddy even knew each other. He caused me to be raised in a godly home by my God-fearing great-grandparents. He caused me to overcome great obstacles and be blessed with the resources to finish college. He caused me to learn about his healing power when I was a very young woman. He opened career doors for me that I did not even know existed. He provided for me when I didn't have a dime. His providence is perfect because he knows exactly when we need to become like his Son. Glory! We need to trust God and obey him. That's the only way to gain the total benefits of his providence, and it's the best way for his purpose to be fulfilled through us.

And just as God's providence is *upon* us, his will is *in* us, doing the work of sanctification. Sanctification is the *grace* of God shaping us according to the *will* of God. First Thessalonians 4:3 says, "For this is the will of God, your sanctification." As we are sanctified, the Holy Spirit gives us the willingness to grow in holiness and submission, and as we grow this way, we take on the image of Christ and become separated from the world's systems. This transformation requires a *daily* act of submission and servanthood in which we die to self and live for Christ. The will of God working in us says that we want to do the will of the Savior; we want him to be the Lord of our life. We want him to be in charge of our every decision, our every action. When we pray, "Fulfill your purpose for me, Lord," and, "Thy will be done on earth as it is in heaven," we have to really mean it, even knowing that his will doesn't always conform to our hopes and dreams.

It takes faith to accept that God's providence is upon us and God's will is in us. We must have confidence in things we cannot see. How often do I have to remind myself that I can't look at things the way they appear but the way God's Word says they *will be*? For example, if my children are not doing the right thing and I begin to agonize about that, I have to go back to God's Word for reassurance. Psalm 72:4 reminds me that "he will save the children of the needy." That verse is talking about *me*, because I constantly need God's reassurance and grace, so I'm definitely needy! Instead of worrying, I need to trust that God is working in the supernatural to carry out his plan for my life and the lives of my loved ones. What is happening now is not the end of the story. I know that, because I know God keeps his promises.

A Faith Sealed in Concrete

Our focus verse for this chapter is one of the strongest assertions of faith we could ask for. It tells us that God *will* work out his purpose for our lives. It's a verse of hope and praise, and a plea for God's continual presence in our lives. Read it again, commit it to memory, and add it to your storehouse of scriptures. It seals in concrete the message of Romans 8:29–30. God has decided that we will become like his Son. He has "called us to come to him." He has filled us with his goodness and given us "right standing." And he has promised us his glory. This is the kind of faith we must pray for daily. This is the kind of mind-set we should constantly contemplate, inviting our Creator God to fulfill his purpose for us.

What's the Buzz?

The LORD will fulfill his purpose for me; your love, O LORD, endures forever—do not abandon the works of your hands.

—Psalm 138:8 NIV

God has a purpose for your life. Don't go buzzing off without him! Whether or not you can see the end result, seek his will and his way by submitting daily to his guidance and by returning again and again to the nourishment of his Word.

4

Perseverance

God Gives Us Gusto

I can do all things through Christ who strengthens me.

—Philippians 4:13

$\mathscr{W}$hen the Women of Faith tour was in Fort Worth several years ago, my co-worker Pat Mays invited her husband, William, to visit the conference and help her work at my products table, selling books and other items. William is a big, burly guy who works in construction and is smart enough and strong enough to do just about anything. So he agreed to help us on Saturday, thinking that working at the products table would be a piece of cake, a little fluff job, especially compared with his construction duties. He agreed to do it as a favor to Pat. No problem. I mean, how hard can it be to stand at a table and sell books and bumblebee pins, right?

Things started out OK as the doors to the auditorium opened that morning and the women started trickling in. But pretty soon the crowd on the concourse grew larger, and the women were in a hurry to get their shopping done and find their seats. At times the concourse was frozen in gridlock, and shoppers were pressed up to the sales tables, having to shout to make their questions heard as they tried to make their selection while the massive flow of attendees crept along behind them. In other words, it was business as usual on Saturday morning at a Women of Faith conference! As the program began, things quickly settled down. Then, during the morning break, the doors swung open and out poured the crowds again, eager to use the restroom, make their purchases, and get back to their seats for the next session.

William had apparently pictured Women of Faith conferences as quiet, demure gatherings. He wasn't ready for, as he put it, "all those crazy women yelling questions at me and throwing money in my face." By the lunch break, Pat looked around, and William was nowhere to be found. She asked if anyone had seen him, but no one had.

Puzzled, she finally decided to call home. William answered the phone. He told her, "Baby, I had to get out of there. I couldn't take it anymore." Then he added, "Pat, you are an even better woman than I thought. I can't believe you do that nearly thirty weekends a year."

William's construction job took him out in the hot sun and the freezing wind, lifting and pounding and blasting and doing who knows what all. He thought he was prepared for anything, but he wasn't prepared for twenty thousand women! The next morning he broke out in hives, his blood pressure shot up, and he was off to the emergency room! Bless his heart, the experience nearly did him in, and it took him awhile to get over it.

Since then, whenever the Women of Faith conference comes to our area, William stays home with his and Pat's twin grandchildren, and her daughters help at the book table. He used to think he couldn't keep the twins—they were too much for him—but his experience at the book table put that challenge in perspective!

William's a good sport for letting me tell this story on him. The truth is, he was uncomfortable working in that stressful, crowded situation at the book table, but if we had really needed him, if it had been a crucial matter to have him there, he wouldn't have left Pat's side. Not for a minute. But in reality, we had enough help, and we were accustomed to the throngs of women and their hurried, loud questions and requests. So it wasn't a big deal that he left.

I like to remember that story, though, whenever I'm about to charge off somewhere and attack a new task or a new challenge that I'm just *sure* I can do. I am a confident person, I know I'm good at what I do, and I believe I can do just about anything I set my mind to. But I also need to remember something else as I'm tearin' out the door on my way to conquer some new challenge. I need to remember the two most important words in the "I can do all things" verse at the beginning of this chapter; those two words are "through Christ."

It's Christ who gives us the strength to do the things that really matter, to endure whatever challenges he sets before us, and to persevere when the hard times come. When we discern God's will in a situation, when we feel him pushing us or leading us to take on a task or accept a challenge, then we pray for him to be our strength in enduring what's to come, and we set out confidently, knowing we'll get the job done. We'll persevere no matter what. I like to say that the will of God will never take us where the strength and power and grace of God cannot keep us.

I've had to cope with some pretty hard stuff during my life. But you know what happens when God repeatedly gives you strength to survive overwhelming difficulties? You learn that when the next difficulty comes, he'll give you strength again to persevere. See it proven true a few times that "I can do all things through Christ who strengthens me," and, girl, you start believing it!

Everyday Strength

Did you know a bee's honey stomach is just a little bigger than a grain of rice? No? Well, that's about the size of it. In her book *Bees,* writer Elin Kelsey says it "may take as many as 1,000 flower visits" to fill that little stomach with nectar. Bees make honey by regurgitating the nectar in and out of their honey stomach to remove the water in it and to mix it with enzymes. To make just *one thimbleful* of honey, says Kelsey, "a single bee probably works ten hours a day for six days straight."

Bees also gather pollen, carrying it back to the hive in heavy pouches attached to their back legs. In his book *The Queen Must Die and Other Affairs of Bees and Men,* beekeeper William Longgood speculates that "gathering the tiny grains of pollen must be a tedious business at best, going all day from flower to flower, taking a speck here, a speck there. But is it any more tiresome or boring than squandering one's days and life juices performing any of the infinite repetitive tasks most humans must do in order to live?"

I know all about the tedious business of making a living through "infinite repetitive tasks." That's how I learned to rely on the Lord's strength for not only the biggest challenges in my life but also the not-so-big ordeals. I had to persevere to get through some really trying or tedious jobs early in my life. One of the first ones was teaching football players to type—and let me tell you, that was no easy task! Not because football players can't learn typing (or keyboarding, as I suppose we would call it today) but because (1) most of them had hands and fingers so big they needed extra-large keyboards, which don't exist, and (2) most of them didn't want to be there in the first place. They weren't planning to make their living by typing!

Believe me, it took a lot of "I can do all things" prayers to get through that job! Just making myself get out of bed every morning and go to work with a smile on my face took supernatural strength! Finally I moved on, landing a job that involved typing orders for a farm implement company. It was an improvement, but soon I was asking the Lord for strength to get me through each day of that repetitive, tedious job.

Later I operated a proof machine at a bank. That sounds pretty important—and I guess it was, when you look at the big picture of how checking services operated back then. The proof machine feeds a check one at a time into a slot so it appears in front of the operator, who then keys in the amount the check is written for. The machine then prints the amount on the check in code so it can be read by other machines without human help as it makes its way through the banking system. Talk about mind numbing! Try typing nonstop numbers for eight hours a day, five days a week, and see how you feel about getting up and going to work in the morning!

In those tedious jobs, I needed emotional and spiritual stamina to endure the everyday boredom that threatened to consume me. I was always thankful to have a job, even a job that I endured but didn't enjoy. Those were jobs where, from the time I got there until the time I left, I counted down the hours, and minutes until going-home time. As I counted down the hours, I silently prayed, recited scripture, and sang praise songs in my mind. Looking back, I can see that those personal worship practices were lifelines that tied me to Jesus's strength, kept my spirits afloat, and helped me maintain a joyful attitude despite the tedium.

Scripture says, "Ask, and it will be given to you; seek, and you will find; knock, and it will be opened to you" (Matthew 7:7). Through that time I kept asking God for strength to endure what I had to endure. And I kept seeking his guidance, and knocking, knocking, knocking, knowing he *would* open it and lead me to a career that would let me fulfill his purpose in me. As I told you back in chapter 3, he did exactly that, but in his own timing and by his own design.

---

bee fact

❖ ❖ ❖

A bee's two pairs of wings make her a powerful flyer, able to buck raindrops almost as large as she is, fly against strong headwinds, and carry loads of nectar equal to her own weight.

—William Longgood,
The Queen Must Die and Other Affairs of Bees and Men

Supernatural Strength

I was working at one of those tedious jobs when I found out I was pregnant with our third child. Under normal circumstances, I could have continued the job; it wasn't physically challenging, and we certainly needed the money. But my pregnancy quickly turned into anything but normal. In fact, my doctor told me my pregnancy was the most difficult one he had seen in twenty years of practice. When I was in my second month, he ordered complete bed rest until the baby was born.

You would think it doesn't take much strength to lie in bed for seven months, but when you're concerned about your baby being born healthy—and about surviving yourself—let me tell you, honey, it takes strength! And keep in mind, I already had two young children and a husband to be concerned about during that time. Plus all those bills to pay, and now we were down to one income. So I needed more than everyday strength. I needed the kind of strong perseverance that only God can enable.

I constantly prayed, praising him for the uplifting hope with which he showered me and also for the "I can do all things" kind of supernatural strength that only he could provide. And ever since that baby's birth, I have thanked God for the miracle he worked so that we both survived. Today Lesa and her older sister, Vikki, travel with me on the Women of Faith tour, creatively expressing their love for the Lord through their beautiful, interpretive dance.

Tedious jobs and a life-threatening pregnancy weren't the only events in my younger days that required supernatural strength. As my dear great-grandmother grew older, her health eventually failed, and she became an invalid, unable to do anything for herself; she was completely bedridden. This was the great-grandmother who had taken me into her home and raised me when my mother became ill and was no longer able to care for me. When I said I wanted to care for Granny myself, the doctor told me I wouldn't be able to do it. Her condition was too severe, he said. Her needs were too great.

My family wanted to put Granny in a nursing home. My sister echoed the doctor's warning. "It's just too much for you, Thelma, too much for any of us. You can't do everything Granny needs to have done for her," she said. Then she added ominously, "Girl, I know how you love her, but if you take on that responsibility, you will lose your mind trying to take care of her *and* do all the other things you have to do. You will lose your mind, I tell you!"

I knew the doctor and my sister were right. In my own strength, I couldn't care for Granny. But I prayed about it, and I sought God's will for the situation, and in the end I knew I couldn't put Granny in a nursing home. She had taken me in when I was two years old, and she had raised me with an abundance of love and invaluable wisdom. She had introduced me to Jesus, and I had claimed him as my Savior at an early age. Granny had raised me in the church—and I mean that literally. We were there seven days a week: Monday night for mission, Tuesday night for women's auxiliary, Wednesday night for prayer meeting, Thursday night for choir rehearsal, and Friday night for teachers' meeting. We helped clean the church on Saturdays, and you know black folks stay in church all day on Sundays. So it shouldn't surprise you that I grew up loving the Lord.

Now I felt like God was equipping me to take care of Granny. He was giving her to me just as he had given me to her when I was a child.

Finding the Strength to Say Good-bye

When Granny's health failed, I faced two impossible challenges: first, I knew I had to care for her somehow, and second, I knew that before long I would have to give her up. The only way I could endure those challenges was to rely on God's strength and not my own. Once again Philippians 4:13 became my constant motto, a reminder to myself that I could do *all* things—even impossible things—through Christ who strengthened me.

Many of you reading this book are familiar with that demanding, difficult, and sorrowful journey toward the impending death of a loved one. The job of caring for an ailing parent or grandparent is made all the more complicated when you're also working full-time and have responsibilities as a wife and mother, as well as a daughter—or, in my case, a great-granddaughter. The days are long and exhausting, both physically and emotionally. Sometimes I didn't have as much time as I wanted to study my Bible, so I was grateful for the storehouse of scripture I had committed to memory. As I've already explained, those verses inspired, encouraged, and energized me as I went about my day.

As I bathed Granny, I remembered the story of how Lazarus's sister Mary had tenderly rubbed Jesus's feet with expensive perfume and wiped them with her hair (see John 12:3).

As I dressed her each day, I remembered the passage from Isaiah that Granny had taught me to love: "He has sent me to bind up the brokenhearted, to proclaim freedom for the captives and release from darkness for the prisoners, . . . to comfort all who mourn, and provide for those who grieve . . . to bestow on them a crown of beauty instead of ashes, the oil of gladness instead of mourning, and a *garment of praise* instead of a spirit of despair" (Isaiah 61:1–3 NIV, emphasis mine).

As I fed Granny, I thought of all the times she had fed me and showered kindness upon me — and a whole lot of other people. Then I would think of Jesus's words to the righteous: "Come, you blessed of My Father, inherit the kingdom prepared for you from the foundation of the world: for I was hungry and you gave Me food; I was thirsty and you gave Me drink; I was a stranger and you took Me in; I was naked and you clothed Me; I was sick and you visited Me; I was in prison and you came to Me."

The righteous people were surprised by his words. They asked, "Lord, when did we see You hungry and feed You, or thirsty and give You drink? When did we see You a stranger and take You in, or naked and clothe You? Or when did we see You sick, or in prison, and come to You?"

Jesus answered, "Inasmuch as you did it to one of the least of these My brethren, you did it to Me" (Matthew 25:33–40).

Granny had taught me the blessing that comes from being Jesus's hands on earth. As I cared for her, I was energized by realizing that what I was doing for her, I was doing for Jesus. It's easier to persevere through difficult times when your work is a labor of love. Still, the work was exhausting, and the days were long. There were times when I thought my sister's prediction would come true and I *would* lose my mind.

It was a situation that perfectly illustrated that essay about looking back and seeing only one set of footprints in the sand. I couldn't have walked through it on my own, so Jesus carried me. I provided all the essential care Granny needed. When she needed to be turned in the bed so she didn't get bedsores, I turned her. I moistened her lips with an eyedropper, massaged her body to keep the circulation going, and I changed her like you would change a baby.

Despite the great demands her care placed upon me, for a long time, I couldn't let her go—couldn't bear the thought that my precious Granny would die. There were even some in my family who said I was being selfish for working so hard to keep her alive. I asked the Lord to help me discern his will, and once again he did. Where once I had been filled with despair anytime I thought of Granny dying, suddenly he gave me a great sense of peace.

On a Friday evening, I held Granny's hand and told her, "If you're ready to go home to Jesus, Granny, then

I'm ready to let you go." At 1 a.m. on Sunday she moved on to heaven. Throughout the time of mourning that followed, I continually asked God to help me persevere through the journey of grief. And he did.

Working without Weariness

Saying that we can do all things through Christ doesn't mean we can suddenly perform impossible physical feats. Don't look for Thelma Wells among the pole-vault contenders at the Olympics! And don't try to stop a train by standing on the tracks! What the apostle Paul was saying to the Philippians in this bit of encouragement was that in Christ we can *endure* all things. We can get through hard times. We can persevere against great odds, because Christ gives us the strength to "keep on keepin' on." We can handle the hard times on earth because we know we're not here to stay; we're just passing through on our way to heaven. The bad times are gonna end, and the good times will begin—if not on earth, then in heaven!

Jesus said, "In the world you will have tribulation; but be of good cheer, I have overcome the world" (John 16:33). When I read that verse, I always get a little surge of joy when I come to that word *but*. You read that first part, and it's pretty heavy; then when you see that word *but*, you know something good's coming on the other side of that word! Jesus said we're gonna hit hard times during our life-time here on earth; tribulations are inevitable. *But* we're gonna persevere. We're gonna make it. We're even gonna be cheerful in spite of our troubles. As the prophet Isaiah wrote of "those who hope in the LORD," we will "renew our strength, . . . soar on wings like eagles, . . . run and not grow weary, . . . walk and not be faint" (Isaiah 40:31 NIV).

Jesus has already overcome the world and has pre-pared mansions for us in heaven. Just think! Our heav-enly palaces are already there, just waiting for us.

I can't wait to get up there and hug my Granny again. Then I'll get fitted for my crown—and maybe some

---

bee fact

❖ ❖ ❖

As a field bee gets old and her wings begin to fray and wear out, when she is no longer able to fly great dis-tances and carry heavy loads, she may be permitted to work inside the hive again, as she did in her youth.

—William Longgood,
The Queen Must Die and Other Affairs of Bees and Men

---

angel wings too. I'm gonna look good in heaven, girl! But in my imagination, I don't picture myself arriving at the pearly gates all dressed up in formal attire. I don't want to look like I've been sitting around for years, not wanting to get wrinkled while I'm waiting for the Lord to come back. I want to look like my Granny's old Bible—dog-eared, marked up, pages smudged, cover faded. I want to look like God has *used* me to do his good work on earth. I want to be able to say, "Lord, I always tried to be the best I could be for you. It wasn't always easy, but I persevered because you always gave me strength."

What's the Buzz?

I can do all things through Christ who strengthens me.
—Philippians 4:13

Meet your next challenge, persevere through the next difficult time "not by might, nor by power, but by my [God's] Spirit" (Zechariah 4:6 TLB). Face it with the attitude of the apostle Paul, who declared, "I can do all things through Christ who strengthens me," and also with the courage of the shepherd boy David, who yelled as he charged at the giant Goliath, "This battle belongs to God!"

5

Prayer

God Speaks Our Language, With or Without Words

Search me, O God, and know my heart;
test me and know my anxious thoughts.
See if there is any offensive way in me,
and lead me in the way everlasting.

—*Psalm 139:23–24* NIV

It was that time of year when Women of Faith conferences were scheduled for several weekends in a row, and it seemed like there was barely time to get home, unpack, and try to catch up on office work and other commitments before we were back at the airport, catching another plane. Some weeks we didn't know if we were coming or going.

On this particular Thursday, I found myself with my

co-workers Pat and Karole at the bustling Dallas–Fort Worth International Airport once again. We scooted out of the backseat of the taxi, gathering our purses, tote bags, computer case, and jackets as our driver lifted our luggage from the back of the car and set it on the curb. Almost before we were out of the car, a friendly skycap came up to us and said with a big smile, "Hello, ladies. Where are you off to today?"

I looked at Pat and Karole, and Pat and Karole looked at me. Then we all turned back and looked at the skycap, who was waiting expectantly, luggage in hand.

"I have no idea," I confessed.

"I think it might be Omaha," Karole blurted out.

"No, that was last week," Pat said, digging through her purse in search of our itinerary. It took a while (digging through Pat's purse is no easy chore, even for Pat!), but she finally came up with the papers. "Nashville!" she shrieked triumphantly.

The skycap looked at us a little suspiciously, probably wondering if we were really capable of traveling without some kind of caretaker accompanying us. But he dutifully checked our bags, and we made it to Nashville just fine, eagerly anticipating another Women of Faith weekend.

We arrived at the hotel and stood in line a few minutes

at the check-in desk. Just as it was our turn at the counter, I turned, looked up toward the far corner of the lobby, and erupted into a head-shaking, lip-flapping, cheek-billowing "Bloobbbaa-bloobbbaa-bloobbaa" while wigglin' like I was pulling on a pair of pantyhose.

Pat, who has been my friend and co-worker for years—in fact we're frequently together seven days a week—sized up the situation and thought, *What everyone has predicted has finally happened. Thelma has had a meltdown. The stress has finally gotten to her, and she has lost her mind, just like her sister said would happen so long ago. HOUSTON, WE HAVE A PROBLEM!*

Other people might have grabbed me and given me a hard shake, trying to bring me back to reality, but Pat, always the levelheaded one, simply turned to the desk clerk and said, "I'm sorry to rush you, but Thelma's not feeling well, and we need to get checked in right away, if you don't mind." In her mind she was thinking, *If we can just get her to the room, Karole and I can probably calm her down and keep her from hurting anyone until Vikki gets here tomorrow. Then she can deal with her mama and get her back to Dallas.*

I was shocked to hear Pat say later that she and Karole thought I had lost my mind. Of course I hadn't lost my mind! (You knew that, didn't you?) But I *had* spotted Big Billy, the Children of Faith mascot, coming down the escalator as it descended into the hotel lobby. I was just greeting Big Billy in his own language. Decked out in a big costume like those mascots that work the baseball games, he greeted audiences that way at Women of Faith and Children of Faith events: "Blooobbbaa-bloobbbaa-bloobbaa!" (It's actually a language that's impossible to spell out in English, so you'll have to use your wild imagination to comprehend just how it looks and sounds.)

---

bee fact

❀ ❀ ❀

Bees cannot hear sounds in the way we do, only as vibrations travelling along a surface with which they are in contact.

—Daphne More, *The Bee Book*
(In other words, they don't ask, "What's the news?" but "What's the buzz?"—TW)

Interpreting a Language beyond Words

My fluency in Big Billy's language is a silly example of a serious promise in Scripture. It's about prayer and how we communicate with Father God. In one of his New Testament letters the apostle Paul assured the Romans (and us today) that "the Holy Spirit helps us in our distress." Then he went on to say that the Holy Spirit helps us even when we don't know exactly what kind of help we need or when our needs are so great we can't even express them in words: "For we don't even know what we should pray for, nor how we should pray. But the Holy Spirit prays for us with groanings that cannot be expressed in words" (8:26 NLT).

Sometimes we feel so low—we're hurting so bad or we're grieving so hard or we're feeling so lost—that we want desperately to feel the Lord's presence in our lives, but we just don't have the words to express the depths of our despair. Sometimes all we can do is whisper again and again that lifeline name of "Jesus . . . Jesus . . . Jesus." That's when the Holy Spirit steps in and intercedes for us in "groanings that cannot be expressed in words." *The Message* interprets the verse this way: "If we don't know how or what to pray, it doesn't matter. He does our praying in and for us, making prayer out of our wordless sighs, our aching groans."

Hallelujah! God speaks our language even if it's one of "wordless sighs" and "aching groans."

Keep that fact in mind when the hard times come and you find yourself desperately reaching out to the Father. You may be unable to articulate the great need that's overwhelming you, but perhaps you can pull from the promise pantry of your mind the focus verse for this chapter and say to him, "Search me, O God, and know my heart; test me and know my anxious thoughts . . . and lead me in the way everlasting." Then maybe you will say, "Know my heart, Lord. Know my anxious thoughts. I can't put two words together to even describe how bad things are right now. But *you* know, God, and I trust you to lead me out of this dark place."

Psalm 91:15–16 describes what happens when God hears our crying, aching, groaning plea for help. (I've changed the following pronouns to make it more personal for us ladies.) The Lord says:

> She shall call upon Me, and I will answer her;
> I will be with her in trouble;
> I will deliver her and honor her.
> With long life I will satisfy her,
> And show her My salvation.

Our Holy Intercessors and Interpreters

Just as the Holy Spirit translates our moans and groans and intercedes with us before God, so he also interprets, or helps us understand, God's will for our lives, convicting us when we do wrong, comforting us when we are sad, guiding us in what we should do. The Holy Spirit moves into our heart the instant we accept Jesus as our personal Lord and Savior, God's always-on-call gift to us and intercessor for us.

Jesus also hears our unspoken cries of the heart and intercedes for us with the Father. He understands what we're going through because he came to earth as a human being and endured the same trials and temptations we face today. That's why Hebrews 4:14–16 (KJV) assures us, "Seeing then that we have a great high priest, that is passed into the heavens, Jesus the Son of God, let us hold fast our profession. For we have not an high priest which cannot be touched with the feeling of our infirmities; but was in all points tempted like as we are, yet without sin. Let us therefore come boldly unto the throne of grace, that we may obtain mercy, and find grace to help in time of need."

Girl, it's time to shout hallelujah! Think of it this way: God not only hears our prayers directly, but we also have these *two* holy intercessors, Jesus and the Holy Spirit, translating our prayers into the language of heaven and whispering them into God's ear. Well, it just doesn't get any better than that!

The Key to the Kingdom

Because it is by prayer that we first claim Jesus as our Savior, it makes sense to think of prayer as the key that unlocks all the benefits and promises and glory of the kingdom of God. It starts with something as simple as praying—and believing—these words: "Dear Jesus, please come into my heart and become my Lord and Savior. I believe that God raised you from the dead and that you, Jesus, live in the world today. I want to be able to fully depend on you to help me in my time of need and to rejoice with me when I'm happy. I receive you as Lord, and I want the Holy Spirit to live inside me, helping me with everything I do. Thank you for accepting me, Jesus, because I fully accept you. Amen."

Oh, I feel another shout comin' on, just picturing a new believer whispering that prayer and being welcomed into the kingdom of God. Hallelujah! Thank you, Jesus!

Now let's put together the fact that Jesus is our intercessor and the additional fact that prayer is the key to the kingdom. Here's how I like to think of it:

I picture myself standing at a door. There's a frosted-glass panel, and I stretch and twist and stand on tiptoe, trying to peek around the frosted portions to see inside the room, but I just can't see anything. I know there's someone on the other side of that door, but I can't see who it is or what's going on in that room. So I knock. And knock. And knock. (Remember Jesus's instructions to us in Matthew 7:7? "Ask, and it will be given to you; seek, and you will find; knock, and it will be opened to you.") Suddenly I remember that I have a key. (As some of the young kids would say these days, "Duh! You *have* the key!") I put it in the lock, and voilà! The door opens.

I find myself in a room so bright I can hardly keep my eyes open. Then I hear the voice, truly the sweetest voice I've ever imagined saying the sweetest words I'll ever hear: "Father, Thelma is calling on you for help today. She's got a problem, and she's asking for your guidance. She has fought a good fight of faith, and she believes you will give her direction so she'll know what to do. She knows she's not always worthy of your help, Father, but she loves you and believes in your Word and wants to do what you would have her do. She is praying to you, praising your name and thanking you for showing her your grace and mercy. She is groaning and crying out to you through the power of the Holy Spirit. She knows you are the God of grace and the God of glory. Her testimony of your touch on her life will be shared with others who will hear and believe."

As I picture this scene, I weep for joy and feel comforted by the miraculous peace that surpasses all understanding (see Philippians 4:7). I know that the voice I imagined is the voice of Jesus himself as he sat at the right hand of the Father making intercession on my behalf (see Romans 8:34). The key that opened the door to heaven was my earnest, heartfelt prayer.

Once again I'm feeling like that little bee who has found a rich supply of flowers and can't wait to get back to the hive to share the good news. I've just shared with you the key to the kingdom! Read this little description of "Dance Directions" from Elin Kelsey's book *Bees* about what happens when bees share the good news and see if it doesn't remind you of how joyful Christians tell others the way to heaven:

The bee does a round dance if the flowers are nearby and waggles for places farther away. As the bee begins to dance, the other bees cluster around her to study her movements, smell the hairs on her body and taste the nectar she has collected. . . . First those closest to the dancer join in the frenzied dance. Soon a long train of bees dance behind the leader to pass the message on. The new bees do not need to follow the dancer to the new flower patch. After they have been given the dance directions, they can make a beeline for the flowers all by themselves.

You don't need Thelma Wells to tell you how to get to heaven. I've already shared the secret and danced out the road map for you. When you pray those simple words, inviting Jesus into your heart, you're ready to make a bee-line straight to the Father!

And one more thing before we leave the beehive: You'll notice that the lesson of the bees also includes the aroma given off by the news-bringing bee. That reminds me of another beautiful scripture that describes how we spread the good news: "Thanks be to God, who always leads us in triumphal procession [I'm thinking that's another term for *beeline*] in Christ and through us spreads everywhere the fragrance of the knowledge of him. For we are to God the aroma of Christ among those who are being saved and those who are perishing" (2 Corinthians 2:14–15 NIV).

How We Pray

Someone has said that "prayer is the heart's sincere desire unspoken and unexpressed." While God hears our unspoken thoughts, there are many times when we are able to—and need to—express prayer in words, either alone or shared openly with others. The New American Standard Open Bible lists four kinds of prayer: secret, family, group, and public.

We've already talked about those secret, unspoken prayers that come out as moans and groans. But we also can pray "secret" prayers of words that we send up silently to God. I like to say that in this kind of prayer your lips aren't movin' but your mind is groovin'! I like to close my eyes and look at Jesus in my mind's eye. There is a sense of comfort and intimacy that sweeps over me when I see him in my spirit.

Family prayer is another form of personal, intimate communication with our Creator. In every family I know, there is someone who's the designated pray-er when the family gathers. My son-in-law teases me that the food gets cold when I pray before family dinners because I go on too long. But I just tell him there's a lot to pray for when I've got the whole gang together under one roof!

The other kinds of prayer in the list, group prayer and public prayer, happen every Sunday in my church. During the service, the pastor asks us to break off into small groups for a few moments so that, in addition to praying publicly, or corporately, as a church, we can also pray individually for each other, being more specific in our praise, thanksgiving, and petitions. That kind of group prayer is also possible in small gatherings like Bible studies or groups of neighbors or friends who gather specifically to pray for one another.

It doesn't matter so much what *kind* of prayer you're praying as that you *are* praying. I used to question what Paul told us to do in 1 Thessalonians 5:17: "Pray without ceasing." I thought that was impossible because I knew we couldn't walk around all the time mumbling prayers. Then I found out what that passage really means: that we're to be in a constant *attitude* of prayer. It's sort of like having radar that's locked on to God's signal so we're in constant "communication" everywhere we go, even while we're doing other things. So now I can confidently say that I *do* "pray without ceasing." I like to say there are two *p*'s in Thelma: prayer and praise. I am an unceasing pray-er and praise-er.

A *Primer on Prayer*

In a city I was visiting, I led a young man in a prayer to receive Jesus as his Savior. Then I urged him to pray every day.

"But I don't know how to pray," he said.

I responded, "Do you know how to *talk*?"

A little shocked at my question, he muttered, "Sure."

"Well," I said, "if you can talk, you can pray. Just open your mouth and tell God whatever you need to tell him. Ask him whatever you need to ask him."

In my opinion, it's much easier to talk to God than it is to talk to a person. Someone like me might take your words and try to tell *you* what you're trying to say. If you're telling me something and you hesitate a second, trying to find the right words, I'm liable to take your thought and run with it, finishing your sentence for you! And while I'm fluent in Big Billy talk, I'm not always so good at mind reading. I may misinterpret what you're wanting to tell me. God won't do that. He never mis-interprets. In fact, he already knows what you're going to say before you say it—but he likes to hear your prayer just the same.

---

bee fact
❖ ❖ ❖

During a heat crisis, field bees may make a hundred trips or more gathering water. . . . The fielders shuttle back and forth from water source to hive, and hive bees race to and fro smearing the dabs of water on the combs. . . . Eventually the hive is cooled down. The crisis is over. The hive bees return to their regular tasks, but no one, it seems, bothers to tell the field bees the emergency is over. They keep appearing with their mouths full of water, looking desperately for someone to take it from them. The busy hive bees ignore them. It is, apparently, a breakdown in communications.

—William Longgood,
The Queen Must Die and Other Affairs of Bees and Men

Not all of us are able or willing to pray in front of others. That's OK. I understand that public speaking, in any form, makes some people uncomfortable—or maybe frozen with fear.

While there's really no right or wrong way to pray, it's

always a good thing to study and research what the Bible says about a subject. God's Word does offer several guidelines and suggestions for how we can make our prayer most effective and most beautiful to God's ear.

For example, consider this list of guidelines:

Psalm 66:18 says we need to pray with purity of heart or "the Lord will not hear."

Matthew 21:22 (NIV) says, "If you believe, you will receive whatever you ask for in prayer."

First John 5:14 tells us to pray "according to [God's] will."

And then there's this parable Jesus used to teach his disciples how to pray with humility and repentance:

Two men went up to the temple to pray, one a Pharisee and the other a tax collector. The Pharisee stood up and prayed about himself: "God, I thank you that I am not like other men—robbers, evil-doers, adulterers—or even like this tax collector. I fast twice a week and give a tenth of all I get."

But the tax collector stood at a distance. He would not even look up to heaven, but beat his breast and said, "God, have mercy on me, a sinner."

I tell you that this man, rather than the other, went home justified before God. For everyone who exalts himself will be humbled, and he who humbles himself will be exalted. (Luke 18:10–14 NIV)

Jesus also taught us to *expect* our prayers to be answered. He said, "Whatever things you ask when you pray, believe that you receive them, and you will have them" (Mark 11:24).

Jesus also gave us an example of how we should pray in what we call today the Lord's Prayer. It's found in Matthew 6:9–13 (KJV):

"Our Father which art in heaven, Hallowed be thy name." We begin by acknowledging God as our heavenly Daddy, and we praise his holy name.

"Thy kingdom come. Thy will be done in earth, as it is in heaven." God's kingdom is not only a place called heaven; it is also something that lives inside of us. His kingdom consists of truth, healing, and all the fruits of the Spirit, as listed in Galatians 5:22–23 (NIV): "love, joy, peace, patience, kindness, goodness, faithfulness, gentleness and self-control." We are asking God to let his kingdom flow through us to benefit other people. And we desire that God's ultimate kingdom come to earth in the form of Jesus the Christ. By asking that God's will be done, we echo Jesus's words to the Father when he faced agonizing death on the cross. In Gethsemane on the night before he died, he prayed, "Father, if it is Your will, take this cup away from Me; nevertheless *not My will, but Yours, be done*" (Luke 22:42, emphasis mine). When we pray that God's will be done, we may not always like what his will means for us—until God's plan becomes apparent for us, either now or when we arrive in heaven and crawl onto his lap and ask him to tell us the story of how our life on earth fit into his design for all creation.

"Give us this day our daily bread." This doesn't mean we're asking for a loaf of Wonder Bread to be delivered to our doorstep every morning (although God did scatter bread over the desert floor to feed the Israelites as they wandered in the wilderness; see Exodus 16:11–18). Instead we're asking God to sustain us with both physical and spiritual nourishment as we do his work on earth, trusting that he will.

"Forgive us our debts, as we forgive our debtors." God forgives us of our sins and does not torment us about them. We are expected to give the same consideration to those who sin against us.

"Lead us not into temptation, but deliver us from evil." Jesus knew firsthand what it was like to be tempted by evil. He warned his disciples, "Watch and pray so that you will not fall into temptation. The spirit is willing, but the body is weak" (Matthew 26:41 NIV). We are asking God to help us avoid those alluring situations and to protect us against sickness, sin, danger, trouble, trauma, and against physical, emotional, psychological, demonic, and other kinds of trouble.

"For thine is the kingdom, and the power, and the glory, for ever. Amen." Only God is sovereign over all the universe. Only God is all powerful. Only God deserves our worship. We must always give him the glory, and then we say, "Amen," which means, "So be it!" "It is finished." "It is done!"

The Power and the Blessing in Prayer

There is power in prayer, and there is blessing. Whether our prayer follows Jesus's perfect model and includes all the elements of full communication with God, or whether it's an emergency SOS—"Oh, Jesus! Help me!"—prayer is our heart's sincere desire to communicate with our Creator. Imagine: The One who holds the universe in his hands also invites us to talk to him anytime we want and tell him whatever we want. Remember, we're told to "pray without ceasing" (1 Thessalonians 5:17). Gladly accepting the invitation, we hand over our burdens into his keeping.

What's the Buzz?

Search me, O God, and know my heart; test me and know my anxious thoughts. See if there is any offensive way in me, and lead me in the way everlasting.
—Psalm 139:23–24 NIV

We can pray by lifting our hearts and hands and voices to heaven while taking others along with us—or we can pray without saying a word, knowing that even our thoughts and the groanings of our spirit are lifted up to God by his Son, our intercessor. Thank you, Almighty God! You are able to do exceedingly abundantly over and above anything I can imagine. Whoooooeeeee! That's a spoonful of honey! I'm getting happy about this. Watch me: I'm going to dance and praise his name. Come on, baby, join me! Glory! Hallelujah! Praise the Lord! Amen!

6

Hope

In the Tunnel of Despair, a Pinprick of Light

Yet this I call to mind and therefore I have hope: Because of the LORD's great love we are not consumed, for his compassions never fail. They are new every morning; great is your faithfulness.

—*Lamentations 3:21–23* NIV

I love that word *hope*. It's a term that brings sunshine into the darkest closet, a promise that brings courage and faith to the hardest situation. It's found in the place where we would least expect it. If you don't believe me, just look where our beautiful focus verse for this chapter is found. Girl, it's in the book of *Lamentations*! If you're like me, you're wondering, *What's an uplifting, full-of-promise verse like that doing in a book full of laments?* But that's the wonderful thing about hope. It pops out in impossible circumstances and sprouts from the worst and rockiest soil. Hope is that pinprick of light that leads us out of the darkest tunnel of despair.

There's an Arabian proverb that says, "He who has hope has everything," and for Christians that is the absolute, no-frills, barebones truth. Because you know what? Our hope is Jesus! And when you have Jesus, baby, you have everything you'll ever need to hang on through the hard times.

Remember that beautiful verse from Isaiah? "Those who hope in the LORD will renew their strength. They will soar on wings like eagles; they will run and not grow weary, they will walk and not be faint" (40:31 NIV). The only problem is that sometimes before we can soar with the eagles, we have to trot with the turkeys!

One of the things my great-grandmother told me again and again as I was growing up was, "Keep your hopes up, girl!" I always tried to do what Granny told me to do, so I've kept my hopes up through some very difficult situations in my life. Sometimes that little thread of hope was all I had to hang on to. But in my mind, that little thread came from the robe of Jesus, the one he was wearing that day when a woman struggled to get through the crowd to touch him.

A large crowd followed and pressed around him. And a woman was there who had been subject to bleeding for twelve years. She had suffered a great deal under the care of many doctors and had spent all she had, yet instead of getting better she grew worse. When she heard about Jesus, she came up behind him in the crowd and touched his cloak, because she thought, "If I just touch his clothes, I will be healed."

Immediately her bleeding stopped and she felt in her body that she was freed from her suffering.

At once Jesus realized that power had gone out from him. He turned around in the crowd and asked, "Who touched my clothes?"

"You see the people crowding against you," his disciples answered, "and yet you can ask, 'Who touched me?'"

But Jesus kept looking around to see who had done it. Then the woman, knowing what had happened to her, came and fell at his feet and, trembling with fear, told him the whole truth. He said to her, "Daughter, your faith has healed you. Go in peace and be freed from your suffering." (Mark 5:24–34)

I can just imagine that woman rushing from her home to meet Jesus and then, seeing the large crowd that followed him everywhere, feeling her heart fill with despair. She had probably hoped to talk to Jesus in private so she could explain her problem, so personal and intimate, and somehow receive healing. Then she saw the throngs of people. She was surely weak due to the continual blood loss. It must have taken heroic effort to push her way through the wild mass of followers. And we know it must have been wild, because look how impertinent the disciples were in answering his question. In modern language they might have said, "Jesus, are you crazy? A hundred people, maybe a thousand, have touched you as we've made our way through this crowd, and now you're asking, 'Who touched me?' They've *all* touched you!"

Yes, it must have been a loud, exuberant mob that surrounded Jesus. The woman couldn't quite make it to the front, couldn't quite catch Jesus's attention. But her hope was so strong it propelled her forward, and in desperation she stretched out her arm and managed to brush his cloak with her fingertips. And because she believed, that was all it took.

---

bee fact

✿ ✿ ✿

Each hair on the bee's fuzzy coat is as sensitive as a cat's whisker. These sensitive hairs help the honeybee to sense what is going on around it, particularly things that it cannot see.

—Elin Kelsey,
Bees

Irrepressible Hope

It doesn't take much to bring hope into play. For the woman in Mark's Gospel, it was the slightest touch of the Lord's garment. For us, it might be the mere mention of his name. The next time you're staring at that brick wall of misery, close your eyes, see his face before you, and let that name fill your heart and your mind: *"Jesus! Jesus! Jesus!"* Then whisper that beautiful verse from Lamentations as your defiant stand against the darkness: "Yet this I call to mind and therefore I have hope: Because of the LORD's great love we are not consumed, for his compassions never fail. They are new every morning; great is your faithfulness."

This inspiring scripture came in the midst of the prophet Jeremiah's pity party when he was ranting and raving and railing, totally upset with God because of the misery of the people of Jerusalem, who were sorely afflicted at that time. Jeremiah was wailing, "Where are you, God? You've turned your face from me. I don't know where you are. Come on, God. Show your face!" Then something stopped Jeremiah. Maybe he felt the *swoosh!* of God's glorious garment brushing by him. Whatever happened, he momentarily ceased his moaning and groaning and somehow tuned in, instead, to the frequency of hope. Here's how *The Message* portrays it:

> I'll never forget the trouble, the utter lostness, the taste of ashes, the poison I've swallowed. I remember it all—oh, how well I remember—the feeling of hitting the bottom. But there's one other thing I remember, and remembering, I keep a grip on hope:
>
> GOD's loyal love couldn't have run out, his merciful love couldn't have dried up. They're created

new every morning. How great your faithfulness! I'm sticking with GOD (I say it over and over). He's all I've got left. (Lamentations 3:19–24)

I know that feeling of "lostness." I know what it's like to keep a desperate grip on hope when God's all I've got left. But—thank you, Father!—God is always enough. When I go back and think about the great things God has done, I am reminded of all the times in the past that Father God has stuck with me and pulled me from the darkness into the light, from the ravishing fire into the refreshing springs of living water. Hope is unsinkable, irrepressible. It's like a beach ball floating on water. You can push it down, but it pops right back.

Remembering God's Faithfulness

Like ol' Jeremiah, I've had experiences in the *past* that instantly remind me *today* of God's faithfulness, filling my heart with hope whenever I find myself in a ditch of despair. Let me tell you about some of those experiences.

Earlier I told you that I was raised by my great-grandmother. Granny didn't really mean to raise me when she took me into her home. She was simply stepping in during a crisis to offer some relief. You see, my mother was an unwed crippled teenage girl who was unable to care for me as she wanted to. At a time when both my mother and I were sick, when I was about two years old, Granny came and got me. She kept me and loved me and nurtured me, and I stayed with her until I married. Then, when she became an invalid, I stepped in and cared for her just as she had done for me.

Sometimes, while I was a little girl, Granny would send me to visit my grandmother, probably thinking that I needed to know and be loved by all my family members. What Granny didn't know was that my grandmother would lock me in a cold, dark, dingy, stinky, mildew-infested, bug-inhabited closet all day without any food or water or conversation or playthings. Grandmother occasionally took in ironing, and she would say she was putting me in the closet for my protection, so that the iron wouldn't fall on me.

I did not realize at the time that she was mistreating me. Inside the darkness of that closet all day, I would sing the hymns I'd learned in church. (Remember how I told you I was there with Granny seven days a week?) At that young age, I didn't know all the words to the precious old hymns like "What a Friend We Have in Jesus," "The Old

Rugged Cross," and "Nearer, My God, to Thee," but I knew the tunes, so I would just make up words for the parts I didn't remember. Being a child, the song I did know was "Jesus Loves Me." Over and over I sang those sweet lyrics: "Yes, Jesus loves me. The Bible tells me so."

I would sing and sing and sing until I sang myself to sleep. Then, when my grandmother opened the door, I walked out of that closet with no bitterness, no anger, no hurt, no harm. I had no idea that what was happening to me was abuse. Nor did I know then that someday, in a tough situation, I would look back, as Jeremiah had done, and I would remember God's faithfulness to me in that closet. I would recognize that those songs of praise I sang in the closet were the thread of hope that wove my heart to Jesus's heart and kept me from becoming emotionally and spiritually scarred by that experience. I needed that protection, because when I got to be a grown woman, I would be called upon to take care of my grandmother for thirteen years. The responsibility was not a burden for me, because I held no bitterness in my heart toward her. "Because of the Lord's great love," I was "not consumed" by anger; therefore I could greet each new day with hope, knowing God's compassion for me—and for my grandmother—"never fail."

God gave me another opportunity to know the "good courage" of hope when I married my husband. As all new brides do, I entered marriage full of hope that George and I would live happily ever after, just like characters in a fairy tale. And we did—for a few days. Then, what a shock, I found out he wasn't perfect. Oh, I had spotted a few deficiencies in him while we were dating, but, as Babbie Mason likes to say, I intended to "raise him up in the way he should go."

It's funny. The things that needed changing in George were very obvious to me, but he never noticed that I needed changing too. I've got to give him credit; that's one fault that was exclusively mine. He kept telling me, "What you see is what you get." But no, my mind was made up. I prayed frequently for our marriage and for George. Mostly I prayed, "Lord, change him!"

Our marriage didn't start off like a fairy tale, and we certainly didn't live in a fairy tale castle. Our first home was a back-alley apartment. When we moved into the projects a little later, that was a step *up*.

I kept hoping things would work out, that we would somehow come to know the kind of marriage I had seen my great-grandparents have, a devoted relationship as strong as the rope symbolized in Ecclesiastes 4:12, which says, "Though one may be overpowered by another, two can withstand him. And a threefold cord is not quickly broken." I wanted George, Jesus, and me to be the three strands making up that strong cord. But to tell you the truth, my strand kept getting all knotted up in itself.

One night when we had friends over to visit, I was busy in the kitchen while George visited with our friends in the front room. He called to me to come turn on the lamp on a nearby table. Well, he could have reached that lamp without even getting out of his chair!

"George, I'm busy. Reach over there and turn on the lamp yourself," I yelled through the doorway.

"Thelma! When I tell you to do something, I expect you to do it!" he replied.

Now, I knew he was just showing off for company. I probably should have just laughed off his remark and gone on ahead with my cheerful dinner preparations. Instead, I came storming out of the kitchen, mad as a hornet, and in no uncertain terms told George exactly what he could do with his arm, the lamp, and his attitude. (I wasn't as anointed then as I am now.)

When the evening finally ended, I got out my Bible, turned to the book of Proverbs, underlined everything a man was supposed to do, and left it lying out for George to see. Unfortunately, at an earlier time I had already highlighted everything Proverbs said a woman is supposed to do. Reading over the marked passages, it was obvious that George wasn't the only one in our marriage who had a few shortcomings!

Years passed, and our flareups continued with increasing frequency. For nearly fifteen years, off and on, I tried various techniques to fix this man, always with the same results (meaning *no* results!).

We weren't living happily ever after, but still, neither of us wanted to give up. We remembered the love that had brought us together, and we remembered the way we had cherished and nurtured each other in the past, and that gave us hope that we would find a way through our difficulties.

Looking back, I wonder if I was a slow learner or just flat-out stupid. Why did I try so hard to make him different? Finally one day in 1974, I reasoned it out. My husband was not the problem. I was. Once I acknowledged my fault, I adjusted my attitude and stopped picking on him. Then came the day when we had a difference of opinion on some trivial matter and George said to me, "I don't like all this arguing. Why don't we agree to disagree and remain agreeable?" And that's exactly what we've done.

Since that day we've never gone to sleep at night angry with each other. That's not to say our marriage has become the fairy tale I dreamed of. The fact is, we've had a lot of sleepless nights! But fairy tales aren't real—and they certainly aren't biblical! There have been plenty of ups and downs in our marriage, but God has helped us find and follow a path of love, mutual respect, and commitment as we have traversed those peaks and valleys. Great is his faithfulness!

Hope is like the towrope at a ski resort that pulls you up the mountainside. The journey is still uphill. There are still bumps and holes to be endured. But if you hang on tight, it gets you where you're going.

Hope in the Demanding Days

Earlier I told you about some of the mundane jobs I held as a young woman just starting out after college. While I was working at the bank, running the proof machine all day long, I continued to hope for a better job. When I got discouraged, I looked back and remembered how God had guided me into my first job and my second, and I held on tight to hope, knowing that if I did my part by being good and dependable at what I was doing, he would be faithful in guiding me to a better job in the future.

---

bee fact

❖ ❖ ❖

Long before signs of spring become obvious in the outside world, a whisper has reached the inmost parts of the hive. The drowsy workers stir. . . . Soon a warmer air will call out the bees to their tasks: some will fetch pollen from the early catkins, some water to dilute the stored honey, so that the increasing host of young can be fed. As the sun strengthens and more and more flowers open, thousands of workers pour out into the bright world to pursue their lives of patient toil.

— Daphne More,
The Bee Book

One day I got up my "good courage" and called the establishment where we did our personal banking. I knew I now had the experience and the credentials to take a step up and claim a better job in the banking business. I asked for the branch manager, Mr. Smiley, and told him I wanted to bring by my résumé.

"That's fine," he answered, "but the bank closes at

three, and it's already two-thirty. You can bring it by tomorrow."

"No sir," I told him. "I'll come right over there, and if I don't make it by three, you can meet me in the lobby of the bank building." (Sometimes, looking back, I can barely believe how bossy I was to my future boss!)

Mr. Smiley met me in the lobby, and I dropped off my résumé. Then I started calling every day, asking if there were any openings. Every day I would be told no. One woman told me, "We have no openings *now* and we expect no openings *in the future.*"

"That's OK," I replied. "You'll call me when something comes up."

I refused to give up hope that God had something better in store for me. I kept calling the bank for weeks—and then months.

One day the bank called me. "We have an opening for a new-accounts clerk," Mr. Smiley said. "The job pays four hundred dollars a month."

I'm sure he expected me to drop everything and hurry on over there to kiss his feet and call him blessed. Instead I huffed, "Mr. Smiley, I ain't gettin' out of bed for no four hundred dollars a month."

"It's all we can pay," he answered.

"That's OK," I said. "You'll call me."

Can you believe I said that? Here I had been begging the man for a job, and when he offered it to me, I turned him down! Amazingly, a few days later he called back.

"Four-fifty?" he asked.

"No," I said. "I'm gonna work hard for you, Mr. Smiley, and I'm worth more than four hundred fifty dollars a month."

"It's absolutely all we can offer you," he fumed.

"You'll call me," I answered back.

A few more days went by, and Mr. Smiley called again.

"Five hundred a month," he barked. "Take it or leave it."

"When do I start?" I meekly replied.

It's funny now to tell that story, but living through it wasn't fun. Applying and interviewing for new jobs can be a hopeful—but also a stressful and uncertain—time of transition. As we go through demanding days of any kind, we need to remember the words of Jeremiah and remember the real source of our hope: God's great love for us. He will not let us be consumed by the struggles of this life. His compassion for us will never fail. It is renewed every morning. So every morning, we arise and greet the new day with hope!

What's the Buzz?

Yet this I call to mind and therefore I have hope: Because of the LORD's great love we are not consumed, for his compassions never fail. They are new every morning; great is your faithfulness.

—Lamentations 3:21–23

God's great love for you will stir up hope in your heart when you're running on empty. When times are hard, call to mind other occasions when God's faithfulness pulled you through, and let his steadfast compassion for you renew your courage and revive your spirit.

7

Faith

Life Is a Roller Coaster,
but Jesus Is My Seatmate

I will repay you for the years the locusts have eaten. . . .Then you will know . . . that I am the LORD your God, and that there is no other; never again will my people be shamed.

—*Joel 2:25, 27* NIV

By now this may not be news to you, but when it comes to new ideas, new opportunities, and new ways to succeed in life, I tend to be bold and energetic. Once I set my mind on something (like getting that job at the bank, as I described in the last chapter), sister, stand back, because I'm gonna try every which way 'til Sunday to achieve my goal. That's just my style. It may not be *your* style, though, and before

I tell you this next story, illustrating how faith has worked in my life, I want you to understand that I'm not saying this is the best way to go at challenges. It was simply *my* way.

We're all created in God's image, yet no two of us are exactly alike. Each one of us is a divinely inspired original. While I tend to be bold and forceful in responding to opportunities, many of my friends are just the opposite, showing more diplomacy and patience. And still others are more balanced, adjusting their response to each specific situation.

I don't know why God made me this way, but I do know that when I get in a tight spot, I start looking up and finding ways to push through. I don't hold back. Not one little bit. Huh-uh. When I sense God's blessing on some project I have in mind, I'm gonna go at it with all I've got until either I've claimed the prize—or the Lord has claimed *me* and hauled me on home to heaven! You'll see what I mean as I tell you how my life's work evolved from a local business to a global career. And you'll see why the verse I've chosen as the scriptural focus for this chapter means so much to me.

"Step Out on Faith"

In the last chapter I described how I talked my way into a job as a new-accounts clerk at our local bank. And earlier I described how my career expanded from that new-accounts job to include teaching American Institute of Banking training classes and seminars based on a book I put together myself. After I started adding that *"bee* the best you can be" pep talk to the training classes, I received invitations to give motivational talks to groups and organizations all over the area.

I worked hard, and soon the bank promoted me. Looking around for ways to expand my responsibilities, I developed a full employee-training program for that specific bank (the AIB classes were for banking employees from throughout the area). Once again I wrote the training book, implemented the program, and soon was given full responsibility for employee training.

In 1978 I became the first black bank officer of a commercial bank in Dallas. Two years later I became assistant vice president of the bank.

So there I was with three jobs, in effect, plus my full-time responsibilities as George's wife and the mother of our three children. I worked Monday through Friday at the bank, taught the AIB training course several evenings every week, and in my spare time did motivational and inspirational speaking. I enjoyed all of my jobs, but I wasn't earning as much as I knew I was worth, and I was wearing myself out! Some days I found myself sitting in the car with the engine running and having to pause a minute until I could remember whether I was coming or going!

It was about that time that my sister Paula started calling occasionally and saying, "Thelma, I want to know how you're *feeling,* but I *don't* want to know what you're *doing.*" She felt overwhelmed whenever I would run through the list of all the things I had going on. It was just too much for her to keep track of, and she worried that I was running myself into the ground—which I was! So she stopped asking about my activities. She just wanted to check in and make sure I was still sane and not lame! As soon as I would tell her I was feeling all right, she would say, "OK. That's good. Bye."

It was also about that time when the idea occurred to me that I should go into business for myself as a speaker. The response to my motivational speaking had been very encouraging, and I began to dream of going into public speaking full-time, using my skills to develop independent bank-employee training programs and to expand my motivational speaking opportunities. The more I thought about it, the more excited I got about that prospect. After a while an urgent restlessness set in. I wanted to leave the bank so bad. I continually sensed that God had placed a greater opportunity in front of me, and I was frustrated that I wasn't being allowed to pursue it. The word *entrepreneur* was being heard more frequently about that time, and I started thinking of myself that way, as an entrepreneur.

But how on earth did a person go about making a living by *speaking*? Just a week earlier I had gotten lost while trying to find a church in Garland, Texas, where I'd been invited to speak. Somehow I had ended up in another Dallas suburb called Flower Mound. I drove and drove and drove, squinting to read the street signs and wondering where I was. Frustrated to think about all the gasoline I was using, I muttered to myself, "I oughta at least be gettin' twenty-five dollars for mileage and all the wear and tear I'm putting on my car." But at most of my motivational speaking appearances, I was compensated only with some heartfelt hugs and thank-yous. To go from that situation to making a living solely off of my speaking abilities seemed like quite a stretch.

Still, I wanted to give it a try. I sensed that God was leading me in that direction, and I had faith that he would guide me every step of the way—if I could just manage to take that *first* step. One day I decided I simply couldn't wait any longer. I had to give it a try. I rushed home to tell George the good news: I was going to leave my banking jobs and set up a business as a full-time business trainer and speaker.

So I told him. And when I did, he took the wind right out of my sails.

"Baby, you can't quit your banking job," he said. "We just can't survive on one income. We've got three kids to feed! There's no telling how long it would take to build up a business like that until it was self-supporting. And where would we get the money to start a business in the first place? I just don't see how we can do it. I'm sorry, Thelma, but I can't let you do it."

It hurt to hear those words, but I knew I couldn't go against my husband's decision. That night I prayed, "Lord, I *know* you gave me this gift of public speaking, I *know* you brought me this idea that's come into my mind, and I *know* you will help me make this dream come true. I put my faith in you, dear Jesus. When it's time for me to take this step, please give the message to my husband."

Well, I expected George to wake up the next morning and say, "Baby, I had the most amazing dream last night! I dreamed you went into business for yourself as a motivational speaker and you were a great success. I'm sorry I held you back. Of course you should do it. I want you to march into that bank today and hand in your resignation."

That's what I *hoped* he would say. But he didn't. Three long years went by, and with each passing month my desire to go into private business as a public speaker increased. But so did George's stubborn insistence that we couldn't afford to take that risk. Still, my faith was strong. I knew without a doubt that the Lord had given me my dream and that he would make a way for me to fulfill it.

One evening as we were flying back from a vacation trip, I sensed the Lord speaking to my spirit, telling me it was time to leave the bank. To be honest, I felt a little put out with God, thinking, *Father, I'm ready! I've been ready for three years. But don't you remember? I asked you to tell my husband when the timing is right. You know I can't go against his wishes. He's got to agree to it. Tell him, Lord, not me!*

I didn't say anything to George.

The next day when I went back to work, my supervisor called me into his office. He told me that the books I'd written for the bank's training courses had become so popular that the bank would like to publish them under its own name and offer them to other banks for training purposes. They would pay me a bonus for this privilege, he said.

I told him I would need some time to think about it. That evening when I told George what the bank wanted to do, he had a one-word answer: "Quit."

"What did you say?" I asked.

"Quit. Tell them you're leaving and you're taking your books with you. You've wanted to do this for a long time. So do it."

"Now?" After all this time of hoping and praying and dreaming, suddenly I felt a completely new emotion: *fear*.

Incredibly, after praying and hoping for this for years, I had a momentary lapse in confidence, wondering, *Can I really do this?* Nervously, I took a yellow legal pad and drove to Wyatt's Cafeteria. I bought a cup of coffee and sat at a table to do what Viktor Frankl describes as "paradoxical intention."

Following Frankl's guidelines, I wrote down my dream of going into full-time public speaking. Then I listed the advantages and disadvantages of making such a career move. I tried to think of the worst thing that could happen if I attempted my dream and failed. Then I thought of the best thing that could happen. I wrote it all down. Next I wrote where I expected to be in my career in five years if I took this step—and where I expected to be in five years if I didn't. Finally I wrote down the answer to this question: "Five years from now, what difference will this choice make for me?"

I sat at the table reading the words I'd written on the yellow pad, then I closed my eyes and prayed. "Father, I feel your glorious presence in this dream of starting my own business," I whispered. "Thank you for being the God of opportunity and encouragement. I sense that you've given me this gift of speaking in a way that inspires and enlightens and energizes those who hear. Help me to use that gift for your glory, Father. Help me to know what step you want me to take. I'm asking in your Son's blessed name. Amen."

I opened my eyes and put down my pen. In my spirit I sensed God saying to me, "You go, girl!"

And he wasn't the only one. Besides God and George, only one other person knew about my dream: my husband's dear Aunt Doretha, mentioned in an earlier chapter. I told her that George had finally given me his blessing to leave the bank. "But now that he says I can do it, I'm feelin' scared, Aunt Doretha," I told her. "It's not like me at all, but that's the truth. I'm scared."

"Baby, step out on faith," she told me encouragingly. "If God ordained it, he will sustain it."

---

bee fact

✿ ❀ ✿

For a new fielder [honeybee], the great adventure begins the first time she leaves the hive to forage and must find her way back. Is she nervous during this initial excursion? Does she keep repeating to herself various landmarks she can identify? Or does she depend on some kind of homing instinct, a route committed to memory or a navigational system known only to her? Whatever the method, it is almost eerie the way she can go two to three miles distant and fly directly to her own hive.

—William Longgood,
The Queen Must Die and Other Affairs of Bees and Men

Walkin' on the Water

Does my story remind you of anyone you know from Jesus's time? For three years I'd been whipped up into a frenzy wanting to leave the bank and go into business for myself. I felt certain God had given me this dream, and I was full of faith that he would help me carry it out. Then the door opened for me, and I lost confidence!

Jesus's disciples behaved like that occasionally. They

were profoundly excited about the Lord's ministry. They had left their lives' work to follow him! They had seen him work miracles. They had heard his profound teachings. They *knew* he was the Messiah. And yet sometimes they had a momentary lapse of confidence. When that happened, Jesus scolded them (or maybe he was teasing them!), saying, "O ye of little faith!" Here's how the King James Version describes one of those times:

When he was entered into a ship, his disciples followed him. And, behold, there arose a great tempest in the sea, insomuch that the ship was covered with the waves: but he was asleep. And his disciples came to him, and awoke him, saying, Lord, save us: we perish. And he saith unto them, Why are ye fearful, O ye of little faith? Then he arose, and rebuked the winds and the sea; and there was a great calm. (Matthew 8:23–26)

I was just like those apostles—fully confident in my faith as long as things were smooth sailing. But let a little storm whip up some waves, and I'm poundin' on the door of the Lord's stateroom begging, "Jesus, save me!"

And then there was the apostle Peter. Bold, forceful

Peter was a lot like bold, forceful Thelma! Another night when the disciples were out on a boat and the winds picked up, they saw Jesus walking toward them *on the water.* Here's what happened:

When the disciples saw him walking on the lake, they were terrified. "It's a ghost," they said, and cried out in fear.

But Jesus immediately said to them: "Take courage! It is I. Don't be afraid."

"Lord, if it's you," Peter replied, "tell me to come to you on the water." [This is the Thelma Wells version of, "Lord, I know you gave me this dream, now please help me fulfill it!"]

"Come," he said.

Then Peter got down out of the boat, walked on the water and came toward Jesus. But when he saw the wind, he was afraid and, beginning to sink, cried out, "Lord, save me!"

Immediately Jesus reached out his hand and caught him. "You of little faith," he said, "why did you doubt?" (Matthew 14:26–31 NIV)

I thought of Peter clambering over the side of that boat

as Aunt Doretha urged me to "step out on faith." And I thought of Peter walking on the waves and losing faith when he suddenly became aware of the storm around him. That was where I found myself at that moment. But then I heard Jesus's question echoing down through the centuries to settle into my heart: *Why do you doubt me, Thelma? O ye of little faith!*

Well, I didn't like hearing those words rattling around my mind! I wanted to show the Lord—and myself—that I was a woman of faith, inside the boat and out on the water!

God's Faithfulness through Good Times and Bad

I left my job as a banker on a Friday, and when I walked out of that building, I was the only one there who knew how to implement the training program I had developed. So I walked back into that same bank on Monday morning as a private consultant and offered a deal they couldn't refuse. For thirty thousand dollars a year, I said, I would come back in for a half-day twice a month and train whomever they wanted me to train. However, if they would pay me for the one-year commitment that day, I would give them a discount and charge them only twenty-seven thousand. The bank accepted my offer, and

I walked out with a twenty-seven-thousand-dollar check, which financed the startup of my company.

With God's steadfast help and a lot of hard work, I developed my skills, built up a clientele, and was soon traveling all over everywhere providing banking and customer-service training mixed in with some motivational presentations. Within a few years I was earning a six-figure income as a public speaker. I was living my dream.

And then it all ended.

The banking industry failed, and so did my banking-related business. Banks started closing, and my clients started canceling. Within six weeks, my income had dropped to *zilch*, *nada*, right next door to *zero*. In fact, that's what it was: ZE-RO.

I didn't panic right away. After all, my husband had a decent income from all the hard work he was putting into the three small automobile-related businesses he owned. Plus, I was well known in the banking industry, and I thought that when those out-of-work bankers got settled in other businesses they would hire me to make motivational presentations to their new employees. But that didn't happen. Instead, I had to rebuild my reputation in those other industries bit by bit.

We went through a seven-year financial drought, during which, in addition to my own setbacks, two of my husband's businesses were forced to close. We were hanging on by the tiniest fiber of faith and the most meager income imaginable. I was on a first-name basis with a lot of bill collectors. They would call about some overdue bill, and I would say, "Hi, baby. How are things in Delaware?" (That's where a lot of credit card companies are based.) I wrote all my creditors, sent in my cut-up credit cards, and promised to pay when I could. And when I did manage to earn a little money, I was careful to keep up my lifelong habit of tithing. When I had so little, it was hard to give any of it away, but I was faithful to God, knowing he would be faithful to me.

But then I started questioning him. (Whining would be a more accurate description.) I said, "Lord, you said if we tithed you would 'rebuke the devourer' for our sake [see Malachi 3:10–11 KJV]. Well, I'm tithing, but I don't see you rebuking nothin'! You said you would give back 'good measure, pressed down, shaken together and running over' [Luke 6:38], but I don't see any good measure. I don't see nothin' pressed down, shaken together, and running over."

Oh, I could work myself up into a good tirade, really givin' the Lord an earful, moaning and groaning about the mess I'd landed in! I did not have a dime to my name, and I wasn't sure how I was going to make ends meet. I was scared! But despite all my complaining, every time I landed in the dumps, the Lord would give me some little gift of encouragement to keep me going.

One day the phone rang; the caller was a woman from the National Speakers Association inviting me to speak at the group's upcoming convention. I was thrilled! What an opportunity it would be to speak at a gathering of professionals who operated speakers' bureaus and organized seminars! But I could hear from the woman's voice that there was a catch.

"The problem," she said, "is that our rules say you have to be an NSA member to speak at the convention. And I can't find your name on our roster."

Don't Do It This Way!

Now, here's where we get to the point where I have to tell you that I wouldn't necessarily recommend that you follow my example here. You're about to see bold, headstrong Thelma in my most creative, confident, faith-clinging form. Some may consider what I did disrespectful, even criminal, but in my heart, I was anything but that. I was—and still am—leaning on the everlasting arms. Baby, I'm always gonna tell Abba God the whole, uncensored truth, and then I'm gonna have faith that he'll work a miracle. Here's what happened:

Knowing I didn't have a dime to my name, I asked the NSA woman how much it cost to join the organization. She said membership dues were $268. That was about $269 more than I had right then! But I asked for her overnight shipping address and confidently told her, "I'll send a check by Federal Express. You'll have it tomorrow."

So I wrote a hot check, and I sent it off by Federal Express. As I dropped the mailer into the FedEx drop box, I prayed, "Lord, if this is you giving me this opportunity, *cover the check*." Then I drew in a long, slow breath and finished the prayer: "If it's not you, Lord . . . let it bounce."

Girlfriends, people end up in jail doing crazy things like this! Frankly, I don't know anybody else who would have handled this situation as I did. (I don't usually hang out with criminal types.) But I know this: My heart was right. I was trusting God regardless of the outcome. And I had faith that he would pull me out of the fire—or walk with me through it!

The next morning—oh, I'm laughing as I write this!—

I found in my mailbox a three-hundred-dollar check from the American Institute of Banking. Attached to it was a note that said, "I was cleaning out my drawer and found this check that belongs to you."

I made a beeline to the bank to deposit the check, singing God's praises all the way. He had covered the check—and had even thrown in money for the FedEx charges!

Next I called my friend Antoinette, who is a seamstress. I told her, "Antoinette, I don't have any money to pay you, but I need a three-piece suit fast. I have some fabric I bought several years ago, but I don't even have thread or a zipper—and I don't have the money to buy them. Could you help me?"

My precious Antoinette said, "Girl, come on over." She made me the suit for free.

Next I called the printer who had done a lot of jobs for me back when I had money. I said, "Mr. Huckabee, I don't have any money to pay you, but could you please print up some invitations for me on whatever paper you might be throwing away after other jobs?" Bless his soul; Mr. Huckabee came through for me too. He printed up invitations to my appearance at the NSA showcase session.

As soon as my membership kit came, I studied the roster and mailed out invitations to every NSA member who sounded like a powerbroker. I wanted to make sure all the important people knew that Thelma Wells was coming to the convention and giving an eight-minute speech. I can't even remember now where I got money for the stamps!

But the plan worked. When I got to the NSA convention, all those important people I'd mailed the invitations to came right up to me like they knew me: "Hi there, Thelma!" "How are you, Mrs. Wells?" "How nice to see you again, Thelma." They thought I'd been an NSA member for years! And when it was time for my showcase appearance, there was a standing-room-only crowd!

I gave it my all, doing my best to show those professional speakers that I was as good as any of them. At the end of my eight minutes, I received a standing ovation. Afterward a man who ran a national speakers' bureau worked his way through the crowd and told me, "I want you to come speak for me."

Now, I had sent all my information to this man several months earlier, asking to be considered for his agency. I hadn't gotten any kind of reply at all. And now, here he stood, telling me he wanted me to join his speakers' group. Two weeks later, I was back at a podium, beginning a rejuvenated career as a public speaker that has continued to this day, including my wonderful association with the Women of Faith conference.

---

bee fact

❖ ❖ ❖

A remarkable thing about bees is how quickly they transform chaos into order. When spilled out on the ramp [in front of the hive] and [the] earth, after being soused with sugar water, they are a squirming, sticky, disorganized mass. Then, out of the confusion a single bee will struggle free and stagger up the ramp, attracted by the smell of the queen and fresh beeswax or honeycomb from the hive, and further drawn upward by natural inclination. . . .

Whether elected, self-appointed, or fulfilling an impromptu role dictated by instinct is not known. But it must take courage or daring to be first, possibly leading the troops into ambush or some other disaster.

—William Longgood,
The Queen Must Die and Other Affairs of Bees and Men

Today, whenever I face a challenge, whenever I find myself stuck in a difficult place, I remember where I've been—and what God has done—and I cling to that promise he made so long ago. It's a promise he has kept again and again and again to his people throughout the centuries: "I will repay you for the years the locusts have eaten. . . . Then you will know . . . that I am the LORD your God, and that there is no other; never again will my people be shamed" (Joel 2:25, 27 NIV). We *will* have difficult times when the bottom drops out and darkness surrounds us, but the Lord our God *will* restore us. And knowing that, we can hold fast to our faith and trust him to make all things work for our ultimate good.

I had seven years of financial trials, but I did not lose my faith that God had called me to this work. I knew in my heart that one day he would restore me to success. And he did. He did for me what this beautiful passage from the Psalms promises:

> Though you have made me see troubles,
>   many and bitter,
> you will restore my life again;
> from the depths of the earth
> you will again bring me up.
> You will increase my honor
> and comfort me once again.
> (Psalm 71:20–21 NIV)

Where Can Your Faith Take You?

As I've told this story, people have said to me, "Thelma, that's a great story, but that's *you*. I could never be a public speaker!" Well, maybe not; I understand that. There are plenty of things I could never do either. I don't see myself ever performing as an acrobat, for example, and I'll probably never become an astronaut. The point is that each of us has gifts, and we need to step out in faith to use those gifts to the fullest extent possible. The Bible tells us, "Each one should use whatever gift he has received to serve others, faithfully administering God's grace in its various forms" (1 Peter 4:10 NIV).

Assess your skills, consider your gifts, then open your mind, think outside the box, and allow God to use you for his glory. Sometimes you have to employ irrational, illogical, possibility thinking to see the opportunities that are out there. (In my case, sometimes you have to be a little bit crazy!) You have to think, *OK, what's the wildest thing I can do to get this done?* Write down every idea that comes to you as you consider ways to implement your goal, then pray over the list and ask God to guide you in discerning his will. Then, baby, climb out of the boat and walk on the water. Step out in faith!

What's the Buzz?

*I will repay you for the years the locusts have eaten.
. . . Then you will know . . . that I am the LORD your
God, and that there is no other; never again will my
people be shamed.*

—Joel 2:25, 27 NIV

The apostle James said, "*Act* on what you hear! Those who hear and don't act are like those who glance in the mirror, walk away, and two minutes later have no idea who they are, what they look like. But whoever catches a glimpse of the revealed counsel of God . . . is . . . a man or woman of action. That person will find delight and affirmation in the action" (1:22–25 MSG). What gifts has God given you to use on his behalf? Don't just sit around talking about possibilities. Find a way to use them for his glory, then step out on faith to put your plan into action.

8

Peace

Bee Anxious for No Thing!

Be anxious for nothing, but in everything by prayer and supplication, with thanksgiving, let your requests be made known to God; and the peace of God, which surpasses all understanding, will guard your hearts and minds through Christ Jesus.

—*Philippians 4:6–7*

$\mathcal{I}$'ve already shared my enthusiasm and insights for some of my favorite passages of scripture that highlight and reinforce our joy, purpose, perseverance, prayer, hope, and faith. Now, as we near the end of the book, I want to focus on what we all want most as we near the end of each day: peace.

Of course we want peace *all* the time in all places—global peace, political peace, civil peace. But even more importantly, we long for personal peace—the kind of peace that "guard[s] [our] hearts and minds through Christ Jesus," as the focus passage so beautifully expresses it. That's the kind of peace that lets us rest easy at night, even when the world around us is anything but peaceful. It's an amazing thing, this kind of peace; in fact it "surpasses all understanding." But it's easy to picture. Just think of all the times you've seen a baby sound asleep in its parent's arms, even when there's great noise or excitement or even danger all around. On television you might see a wildly exuberant political rally, and suddenly the camera zooms in on an infant, sound asleep on its father's shoulder, head jostling as the father enthusiastically cheers for the candidate. Or maybe you've seen youngsters sleeping soundly, curled up in a seat with their head on Mom or Dad's lap, at a sports event while all around them the crowd goes wild with excitement as the competition rages. Another image that comes to mind is a youngster strapped into a safety seat in the backseat of the family car, sleeping contentedly while, in the front seat, the parents are white-knuckling it through an unexpected ice storm that turned a pleasant winter outing into a nightmare experience.

Surely that's the kind of personal peace we all long for: trusting, childlike peace, a mentality in which we feel totally protected. Fortunately, it's the kind of peace God offers us when we make our requests known to him. As adults, we don't get to sleep through the crises that affect us, but we can call upon God's great power and mercy to give us confident, incomprehensible peace in the midst of a life storm, whether it's a minor shower of inconvenience or a whirlwind of devastating loss. In that state of inner peace we're able to connect more securely to God's guidance and protection so that we can endure, and even be levelheaded leaders, as we ride out the storm.

Peace in Minor Irritations and Major Losses

We all want that state of inner peace, but, at least in my life, there always seems to be something trying to keep me from having it. Sometimes I'll get all worked up about something and *then* I remember to turn it over to the Lord. How sad it is, when we are confronted by problems, that we think of asking him for his peace *last* rather than *first*.

Most recently it was my computer that caused me to part with my peace. For more than ninety minutes one night I repeatedly tried to check my e-mail, but whenever the computer dialed the service provider's number, up popped an error message: "Cannot find server."

I didn't really know what a "server" was, but I couldn't help but muse, *Well, why not? You found it an hour ago when everything was working fine. Couldn't you just go back and look in the same place? It can't have gone far.*

Either the server had left the building or the computer wasn't looking in the right place, because they never did connect. In frustration, I gave up and went to bed, hoping they would somehow find each other overnight. The next morning, I turned on the computer, dialed the service provider, and *voilà!* there was my e-mail. But an hour later when I tried to check it again, the computer and the server had once again parted ways: "Cannot find server," it whined repeatedly in the error-message box.

With my frustration rising, I tried to make a phone call on the line my computer is connected to, and I got another annoying message: "We are unable to complete your call as dialed. Please hang up and try again. Message 14XM9" (or whatever).

By this time, smoke was coming out of my eyes. Looking for someone to blame, I decided my husband had forgotten to pay the phone bill. Instantly, I was angry.

Furiously I dialed his number on my cell phone. But he assured me all the bills had been paid on time, as usual.

Next I tried the long-distance company, thinking somehow this could be their fault. A recorded message told me, "We're sorry. We are unable to serve you at this time. Please call back later."

I slammed down the receiver and drew in a deep breath, wishing there was someone I could yell at. But I was alone in the house. I sat there a moment alternately glaring at the computer and the telephone, and finally I realized that my feelings of frustration weren't accomplishing anything. My anger wasn't helping anything either. And my desire to unload on the next person who walked in the door certainly wasn't going to achieve anything beneficial. When I'd run through my list of "options," I eventually got to what I should have thought of first: *Be anxious for nothing, Thelma. In everything—ev-ry-thing—by prayer and supplication, with thanksgiving, let your requests be made known to me; I am the God of peace, and my peace, which surpasses all understanding, will guard your heart and mind from needless anxiety, through Christ Jesus.*

Instantly I felt better. At least I felt less angry and frustrated. But I did feel pretty silly to have let a mindless computer rob me of my peace.

When you hit a wall and there's nothing else to do, do the right thing! Ask God for help. (When you hit the wall, do that *first*, if you can wade through your emotions to think of it.) Don't be anxious, and don't worry. Neither can make things better. But God can. He can give you peace.

Taking Peace Apart

Many years ago I memorized several powerful verses from Philippians 4, including the ones at the beginning of this chapter; again and again they have worked like the balm-of-Gilead to soothe my worries when I get all riled up. So I don't really have an excuse for not calling them to mind whenever worries and frustration start oozing into my mind. To be honest, it's frustrating for me that I get so frustrated when God's peace is so near and all I have to do is connect with him and make my request known to him—but I don't think to do that!

In the best of times, when problems occur, I whirl the Philippians 4 passage through my mind like an audiotape on fast forward. When I do it out loud, I sound like a combination of Mickey Mouse and the announcers who make car commercials. You know the ones: they describe very clearly the big discounts the dealer is offering, and they say the dealer's name nice and slow so you can understand it. But at the end of the commercial when it comes to the terms and conditions of the breathtaking deal, they talk so fast that the details run together into one long multisyllable word. That's the way I "replay" this passage as the pressure is mounting. It's as though I'm rushing to push away my worries with the soothing reassurance of those beautiful words. Then, as the situation eases a bit, I can slow down and appreciate the individual words. Oh, how good they are!

"Be anxious for nothing." Sometimes we misuse the word *anxious* when we really mean *eager*. *Anxious* and *anxiety* have the same root and both mean "to worry." So when we say we're anxious for the dessert cart to come, we really mean we're *eager* for the double-fudge, caramel-pecan torte to make its appearance. Later we may be *anxious* when we have to step on the scales at the doctor's office. Being anxious means our mind is disturbed by real or imaginary fears.

Next look at that word *nothing,* and you'll see two smaller words: *no thing.* Be anxious for *no thing.* Did you get that? No computer. No traffic. No irritating situation. No worrisome trial. No thing. A couple of years ago, I produced some magnets that said, "BEE anxious for No Thing!" There is not one incident, person, assignment, schedule, desire, daydream, condition, affliction, or deadline that will be improved one tiny bit by worrying over it. Yet millions of us are unable to sleep at night or eat breakfast in the morning because we use that time to worry. The Bible tells us to stop worrying—and here's how we do it . . .

"But in everything . . ." Remember what I said back in chapter 4 about that word *but*? When you're reading along and you see that word *but*, you know something good's comin' up! And there it is: "*by prayer*"—that's "the heart's sincere desire, unspoken and unexpressed." And do you remember back in chapter 5 we talked about how you don't even have to pray to pray? Even if your anxiety has you so twisted up in knots that all you can do is make unintelligible noises—"Mmmmm, mmmmmmm, mmmmmm, ohhhhhh, ohhhhhhhh!"—the Holy Spirit interprets your groans and moans to the Father, who bends down to hear and reaches out to help.

". . . and supplication . . ." Now, *supplication* was a word I had to look up. It means "a humble prayer; an earnest entreaty; begging." Depending on the state of our anxiety, that may or may not come easily. If we're so angry we could launch a nuclear attack at someone or something, it may take a little time to calm down enough to be humble, but the Bible says that's what we have to do. If we've been wronged, we may want to screech, "It's her fault, Lord! She caused this mess. Strike her down, Lord!" Instead, we need to whisper the instructions again and again until they finally penetrate through the hard shell of our heart and mind: "Be anxious for nothing . . ." To ease our anxiety, we need to be humble instead of horrible toward each other.

And we're to pray "with thanksgiving." Now, nobody is thankful to be sick or broke or to have a bad diagnosis or a broken relationship. That's not what this directive means. We're to pray with thanksgiving because we know God is going to bring us peace.

You can be thankful because you know that before the foundation of the world, before a single star hung in the sky, before the land divided the waters, God had you on his mind. And he had already solved your problem. Now he's just waiting on you to give it to him.

The next part of the passage tells us to "let [our] requests be made known to God." So many times throughout the Bible, God invites us to bring our problems to him.

For example, in the Old Testament book of Jeremiah, we read, "For thus says the LORD: . . . I know the thoughts that I think toward you, . . . thoughts of peace and not of evil, to give you a future and a hope. Then you will call upon Me and go and pray to Me, and I will listen to you. And you will seek Me and find Me, when you search for Me with all your heart" (29:10–13).

In the New Testament, Jesus said, "Come to Me, all you who labor and are heavy laden, and I will give you rest" (Matthew 11:28). So we let our requests be made known: "Help me, Lord! I'm losin' it! I need your peace, Father. Give me some patience and peace, Father, please." And we *don't* add, even if we really, really want to, "and hurry up about it!"

When we ask, a wonderful thing happens: "the peace of God, which surpasses all understanding, will guard [our] hearts and minds through Christ Jesus."

Girlfriend, the peace that surpasses all understanding is there for the asking! It's as near as your next breath. The next time your emotions threaten to spill over, the next time some fool is standin' on your last nerve, try to keep your wits about you long enough to breathe in a humble prayer, letting God know that you desperately need his help. (Of course he knows this already, but he loves to be asked.) By the time you let out that breath you can feel assured that he is making your request a priority and thinking thoughts of peace for you to keep your heart and mind from imploding.

Now, I know this peace is available, but occasionally I fail to follow the Lord's (and my own) advice. But I'm learning. When my computer misbehaved and went AWOL to look for the server, I struggled with some anxiety, but eventually I remembered to ask the Lord for peace.

Sharing Peace

It's interesting to see how contagious peace can be. And it's powerful too. One person who demonstrates peace during a hopeless or heated situation can reverse the direction of an escalating trial. One person who is filled with God's peace can bring hope to a friend who's drowning in despair or ease the anxiety of a room full of worriers.

When our daughter found some just-right lake property in a beautiful area of Texas, she saved and dreamed and planned, and eventually she was ready to build a home on that land. She designed the house herself. It would be three stories tall with four beautiful terraces and straight-up sides containing doors and windows on all sides. It looked wonderful on the blueprints, and the builders confidently set to work. But within a few weeks they ran into a number of situations they were not accustomed to handling; the unique design of the structure posed new challenges for them. They were having trouble finding the room they needed for all the electrical and phone lines, the plumbing pipes, and all the other utilities necessary in a house.

---

bee fact

❖ ❖ ❖

One researcher now claims that bees have their own form of loafing or resting; after a foraging trip, he says, a field bee crawls into an empty cell [of the honeycomb] and snugs in for a half-hour siesta; she is quiet but it is not known if she is asleep . . . or merely resting. Upon arousing herself, apparently refreshed, she again takes off for the fields.

—William Longgood,
The Queen Must Die and Other Affairs of Bees and Men

The job was about one-third done when it was determined that the builder was not going to be able to finish the job. Imagine our daughter's despair. Here was her dream home, only partially completed, and the builder was out of the picture. She couldn't finish it herself, and if something didn't happen pretty quickly, the bank holding her mortgage was going to get involved. As she tried to figure out what to do, I saw disillusionment, discouragement, and disappointment in her eyes—everything but peace. I prayed lots of "be anxious for nothing" prayers with her and for her as she turned to God for guidance, wisdom, and peace in this difficult situation.

God is so good. He made an amazing way out of that dilemma. In casual conversation with a man in a store, our daughter mentioned her dilemma and how she needed to find a contractor who could help her out of the mess she found herself in. The man highly recommended a builder who had worked for him for years. She contacted this builder and showed him the unfinished dream house.

He looked at the plans, analyzed the problems, assessed the challenges, and told her this: "If you give me the job, you'll be able to sleep peacefully. I won't leave you until it is right."

For my daughter, that man's words were like a spoonful of honey. He offered her not only his carpentry skills but also his understanding. He knew she was worked up about the problems that had arisen. And he knew just the right words to put her mind at ease.

Granny would have called this man "a ram in the bush." The phrase comes from the story of Abraham as told in Genesis, the first book of the Bible. Earlier I shared how Abraham and Sarah became parents at a very old age. After giving them such a blessing, it seems confusing to learn that later God called upon Abraham to give up this precious son in order to test Abraham's faithfulness. He told Abraham to take Isaac up into the mountains and sacrifice him as a burnt offering, following the custom Abraham normally would have carried out with a lamb. It must have been a terribly difficult trip for Abraham as he led his innocent, young son up the mountain trail, carrying the knife with which he would slay the boy and the coals that would light the fire; Isaac carried the wood, not knowing it was to be the fuel for his own sacrifice.

At one point, young Isaac said, "The fire and wood are here, . . . but where is the lamb for the burnt offering?"

Abraham couldn't bring himself to tell his son the truth. He said simply, "God himself will provide the lamb for the burnt offering, my son" (Genesis 22:7–8 NIV).

At the appointed place, Abraham bound Isaac, placed him on the altar they had built, and raised the knife to slay his son. But suddenly the angel of the Lord intervened, telling Abraham, "Now I know that you fear God, because you have not withheld from me your son, your only son" (Genesis 22:12 NIV).

Then Abraham looked up and noticed a ram in a nearby thicket. Its horns were tangled in the limbs of a bush so it could not get away. Abraham sacrificed the ram as a burnt offering instead of his son. And afterward, he called that place "The LORD Will Provide." (Granny would have named it with her favorite saying: "God Will Make a Way.")

Abraham surely couldn't imagine, as he climbed that difficult mountain, why God would demand so much of him. But when he showed his faithfulness, God told him, "Because you have done this and have not withheld your son, your only son, I will surely bless you and make your descendants as numerous as the stars in the sky and as the sand on the seashore. Your descendants will take possession of the cities of their enemies, and through your offspring all nations on earth will be blessed, because you have obeyed me" (Genesis 22:16–18 NIV).

When we are faithful to God during the bad times as

well as the good times, he provides a "ram in the bush," as Granny would say, to meet our needs. The thought gives us peace when we face difficult times. My daughter prayed constantly for God to lead her through the difficulty experienced with the unfinished house, and in answer to her prayers, he provided a contractor who finished her beautiful home. She turned the job over to him, and although it took six months longer than originally planned, throughout those six months as the carpenter worked to solve all the problems in the home's design, our daughter was able to sleep peacefully, just as he had assured her she would. As someone said, peace is the best sleeping pill there is!

bee fact

❖ ❖ ❖

Generally bees are thoroughly oriented to one tiny spot on this earth that is home. . . . Home is a compelling concept for most species, a refuge of safety in an often perilous world.

—William Longgood,
The Queen Must Die and Other Affairs of Bees and Men

Peace Is Precious

What a wonderful thing peace is! This precious gift from our gracious and loving God can soothe and comfort us in the midst of the harshest, most trying situations. It doesn't necessarily fix things; in fact things might just go on ahead and get worse! But God's peace can help you survive the dark times.

When I've had problems in relationships, when I was refused admission to a school simply because of the color of my skin, when I was a little girl locked up all day in my grandmother's dark closet, I knew peace—because I knew Jesus. I had asked him to be Lord of my life when I was four years old. That's what I said: four years old, and I knew exactly what I was doing. Granny had created an environment for me that set the stage for my spiritual development. She reared me in a praying household, a churchgoing household, a household that did not doubt the ways of God. My thoughts were constantly on God, even as a child, and as I filled my mind with him, he fulfilled in me the words of Isaiah 26:3 (NIV): "You will keep in perfect peace him whose mind is steadfast, because he trusts in you." In the closet—and in dozens of imperfect places since then—he has kept me in perfect peace.

The story of Horatio Gates Spafford certainly illustrates how God's peace can flow into and through us in times of trouble and tragedy. In the 1800s, Horatio was a successful Chicago businessman. He was grieving over the death of his young son in 1871 when yet another calamity occurred: a tremendous fire roared through the city of Chicago, destroying hundreds of homes and businesses, including Spafford's.

Hoping to find solace for their grief, the Spaffords planned a trip to England, where they hoped to attend revival services being held by their friend, evangelist Dwight Moody. Mrs. Spafford and the couple's four daughters went on ahead; Horatio would follow later. But before he could sail, his wife and daughters' ship collided at sea with another ship. More than two hundred passengers died. Shortly afterward, Spafford received a heartbreaking, two-word telegram from his wife: "Saved alone."

Horatio sailed on the next ship, rushing to join his distraught wife. After the ship's captain pointed out the place where the ships were thought to have collided, Horatio was filled with an unexplainable—and unsurpassable—sense of peace. Realizing and appreciating the amazing gift he'd been given in the midst of overwhelming loss and grief, he began writing a hymn that has brought peace to millions in the nearly 135 years since then:

> When peace like a river attendeth my way,
> When sorrows like sea-billows roll;
> Whatever my lot, Thou hast taught me to say,
> "It is well, it is well with my soul."

Whether peace is running through my life like a river or sorrows are rolling over me like a stormy sea, those beautiful words resonate through my heart and mind and sweep over my spirit. They remind me that God is near. He says, "I'm with you in your pain, your sorrow, your agony. I'm with you in your divorce, when you have a bad diagnosis, when you lose someone dear to you, when you're fired. I'm with you when your house burns down and your money's used up. I am with you in every situation. I will give you peace . . . if you choose to accept it. Do you want my peace? Or do you want to stay in the middle of your mess and drown in it?"

Use God's Word to remind yourself that this gift is always available to you. Hear him say to your spirit, "Today is your day of release. I have prepared for you this day, this very hour, healing and deliverance from anxiety. Be anxious for nothing—for NO THING."

Jesus is the King of kings, the Lord of lords, and the Prince of Peace. He can do anything, and he chooses to share our burdens and grant us peace. Hallelujah!

What's the Buzz?

Be anxious for nothing, but in everything by prayer and supplication, with thanksgiving, let your requests be made known to God; and the peace of God, which surpasses all understanding, will guard your hearts and minds through Christ Jesus.

—Philippians 4:6–7

As one of my Women of Faith buddies likes to say, there is something wrong with everything and everybody. When things and people go wrong, our peace tends to go right along with them. When you feel yourself sliding over the brink into anxiety, say again the beautiful words of Philippians 4:6–7, and *bee* anxious for no thing!

9

Now, What Were Those Seven Scriptures Again?

$\mathcal{I}$ hope you've enjoyed sharing seven of my favorite Scripture passages, and I hope you'll hide them in your heart, copy them to your memory, save them to your "hard drive," and maybe even, as the ancient Hebrews were directed to do, "write them on the doorposts of your house and on your gates" (Deuteronomy 6:9). Then *use* them. Take them down out of your scriptural pantry and let the wonderful words of God be your guide, your re-assurance, your hope, and your blessing. To make it easier for you, I'll repeat the verses here in one handy honey-comb. Let's dance through these beautiful passages one more time like honeybees showing their hive mates the way to the flower field.

Joy

He will yet fill your mouth with laughter and your lips with shouts of joy.

—Job 8:21 NIV

Purpose

The LORD *will fulfill his purpose for me; your love, O* LORD, *endures forever—do not abandon the works of your hands.*

—Psalm 138:8 NIV

Perseverance

I can do all things through Christ who strengthens me.
—Philippians 4:13

Prayer

Search me, O God, and know my heart; test me and know my anxious thoughts. See if there is any offensive way in me, and lead me in the way everlasting.

—Psalm 139:23–24 NIV

Hope

*Yet this I call to mind and therefore I have hope:
Because of the LORD's great love we are not consumed,
for his compassions never fail. They are new every
morning; great is your faithfulness.*

—Lamentations 3:21–23 NIV

Faith

*I will repay you for the years the locusts have eaten.
. . . Then you will know . . . that I am the LORD your
God, and that there is no other; never again will my
people be shamed.*

—Joel 2:25, 27 NIV

Peace

*Be anxious for nothing, but in everything by prayer and
supplication, with thanksgiving, let your requests be
made known to God; and the peace of God, which surpasses all understanding, will guard your hearts and
minds through Christ Jesus.*

—Philippians 4:6–7

Credits

❖ ❖ ❖

The "Bee Facts" in this book are taken from the following sources:

Elin Kelsey, *Bees*, Nature's Children Series (Danbury, CT: Grolier, 1986).

William Longgood, *The Queen Must Die and Other Affairs of Bees and Men* (New York: Norton, 1985).

Daphne More, *The Bee Book: The History and Natural History of the Honeybee* (New York: Universe Books, 1976).

About the Author

✤ ✤ ✤

Thelma Wells is president of A Woman of God Ministries in Dallas, Texas, where she mentors women in the ways of Christ. She has a Masters in Pastoral Ministry and is the author of several popular books, including *What's Going on, Lord?* and *God Will Make a Way*. She is a key speaker for the Women of Faith® Conferences, where she has ministered to nearly two million women.

EXTRAORDINARY*faith*

CONFERENCE 2005

2005 EVENT CITIES & SPECIAL GUESTS

**NATIONAL
CONFERENCE
LAS VEGAS, NV**
FEBRUARY 17-19
Thomas & Mack Center

**NATIONAL
CONFERENCE
FT. LAUDERDALE, FL**
FEBRUARY 24-26
Office Depot Center

SHREVEPORT, LA
APRIL 1-2
CenturyTel Center
*Sandi Patty,
Chonda Pierce,
Jennifer Rothschild*

HOUSTON, TX
APRIL 8-9
Toyota Center
*Kristin Chenoweth,
Natalie Grant,
Jennifer Rothschild*

COLUMBUS, OH
APRIL 15-16
Nationwide Arena
*Avalon,
Kristin Chenoweth,
Nichole Nordeman*

BILLINGS, MT
MAY 13-14
MetraPark
*Sandi Patty,
Chonda Pierce,
Jennifer Rothschild*

PITTSBURGH, PA
MAY 20-21
Mellon Arena
*Natalie Grant,
Nichole Nordeman,
Chonda Pierce*

KANSAS CITY, MO
JUNE 3-4
Kemper Arena
*Natalie Grant,
Chonda Pierce,
Jennifer Rothschild*

ST. LOUIS, MO
JUNE 17-18
Savvis Center
*Avalon,
Nichole Nordeman,
Chonda Pierce*

**CANADA &
NEW ENGLAND
CRUISE**
JUNE 25 – JULY 2
Tammy Trent

ATLANTA, GA
JULY 8-9
Philips Arena
*Natalie Grant,
Sherri Shepherd,
Tammy Trent*

FT. WAYNE, IN
JULY 15-16
Allen County War
Memorial Coliseum
*Sandi Patty,
Chonda Pierce,
Jennifer Rothschild*

DETROIT, MI
JULY 22-23
Palace of Auburn Hills
*Sherri Shepherd,
Tammy Trent,
CeCe Winans*

WASHINGTON, DC
JULY 29-30
MCI Center
*Natalie Grant,
Nichole Nordeman,
Sherri Shepherd*

SACRAMENTO, CA
AUGUST 5-6
ARCO Arena
*Avalon,
Kristin Chenoweth,
Tammy Trent*

PORTLAND, OR
AUGUST 12-13
Rose Garden Arena
*Kristin Chenoweth,
Natalie Grant,
Tammy Trent*

DENVER, CO
AUGUST 19-20
Pepsi Center
*Avalon,
Kristin Chenoweth,
Nichole Nordeman*

DALLAS, TX
AUGUST 26-27
American Airlines Center
*Avalon,
Kristin Chenoweth,
Nichole Nordeman*

ANAHEIM, CA
SEPTEMBER 9-10
Arrowhead Pond
*Avalon, Chonda Pierce,
Tammy Trent*

PHILADELPHIA, PA
SEPTEMBER 16-17
Wachovia Center
*Kathie Lee Gifford,
Natalie Grant,
Nichole Nordeman*

ALBANY, NY
SEPTEMBER 23-24
Pepsi Arena
*Sandi Patty,
Chonda Pierce*

HARTFORD, C*
SEPT. 30 – OCT.
Hartford Civic Cen
*Sandi Patty,
Chonda Pierce,
Tammy Trent*

SEATTLE, WA
OCTOBER 7-8
Key Arena
*Sandi Patty,
Chonda Pierce,
Jennifer Rothschild*

DES MOINES, I
OCTOBER 14-15
Wells Fargo Arena
*Sandi Patty,
Chonda Pierce,
Jennifer Rothschild*

ST. PAUL, MN
OCTOBER 21-22
Xcel Energy Cente
*Sandi Patty,
Chonda Pierce,
Jennifer Rothschild*

CHARLOTTE, N
OCTOBER 28-29
Charlotte Coliseum
*Sandi Patty, Beth Mo
Sherri Shepherd*

OKLAHOMA CITY,
NOVEMBER 4-5
Ford Center
*Kristin Chenoweth
Sandi Patty,
Chonda Pierce*

ORLANDO, FL
NOVEMBER 11-1
TD Waterhouse Cen
*Avalon,
Chonda Pierce,
Tammy Trent*

1-888-49-FAITH womenoffaith.com

*Guests subject to change. Not all guests appear in every city. Visit womenoffaith.com for
details on special guests, registration deadlines and pricing.*